SPIRIT BOOK WORD

SPIRIT BOOK WORD

AN INQUIRY INTO LITERATURE & SPIRITUALITY

J.S. Porter

© 2001 Novalis, Saint Paul University, Ottawa, Canada

Cover: Allegro 168inc.
Layout: Caroline Gagnon

Business Office:
Novalis
49 Front Street East, 2nd Floor
Toronto, Ontario, Canada
M5E 1B3

Phone: 1-800-387-7164 or (416) 363-3303
Fax: 1-800-204-4140 or (416) 363-9409
E-mail: novalis@interlog.com

National Library of Canada Cataloguing in Publication Data

Porter, J. S., 1950–

    Spirit book word : an inquiry into literature & spirituality

ISBN 2-89507-170-5

    1. Spirituality in literature. I. Title.

PN56.S7P67 2001   809'.93382914   C2001-903067-3

Kristjana Gunnars' untitled poem on pages 73-74 is reprinted from *Carnival of Longing* by permission of Turnstone Press, Winnipeg. All rights reserved.

Poetry by Dennis Lee is reprinted by permission of the author.

Printed in Canada.

All rights reserved. No part of this publication may be reproduced, stored in a retrieval system, or transmitted in any form, or by any means, electronic, mechanical, photocopying, recording, or otherwise, without the written permission of the publisher.

We acknowledge the financial support of the Government of Canada through the Book Publishing Industry Development Program (BPIDP) for our publishing activities.gram (BPIDP) for our publishing activities.

For
my mother and father
my wife, Cheryl
and
my friend Mark Garber
(1928–2000)

The moment you find your magic word…then you have the key, you can start writing.
\hfill *Hélène Cixous*

Sometimes everything starts with just one word.
\hfill *Clarice Lispector*

Our world is a voice, a sob, and a few holy words.
\hfill *Edmond Jabès*

Contents

	Preface 11
I.	Spirit Book Word 17
II.	Love: Raymond Carver 33
III.	Small: Kristjana Gunnars 51
IV.	Revelation: Flannery O'Connor 65
V.	Quick: D.H. Lawrence 79
VI.	Strange: Clarice Lispector 93
VII.	Zero: Emily Dickinson 109
VIII.	Being: Martin Heidegger 123
IX.	Tremendum: Dennis Lee 139
X.	Obedience: George Grant 157
XI.	Mercy: Thomas Merton 175
XII.	Whither the Word? 189
	Ten Good Reads 205
	Acknowledgements 207

Preface

Forgive me. I want to violate silence and talk awhile. I want my talk to be small and strange and obedient. Light too. Light as a Chablis. Light as an Italian cookie. Can I even come close to that degree of lightness? Light as a David Milne brushstroke.

I want a quiet voice, a little voice, a whisper, for I'm telling you a secret I'm not quite sure of myself. A secret I can spoil by a wrongful telling. Will you listen? I have a story to tell—a story of my relationship with ten words and the writers who bring them to flesh, a story of my stutter to pronounce my own lifeword.

Ten words in my daily wordsqualls began to take shape and stand out. Each one I discovered in books; each was charged with spirit. I found the words in the cells of my body and in the lustrous shining within the bodies of others. Maybe, with these ten spirit-words, I've inadvertently drawn my own face, the geography of my own soul.

On days of euphoria, I think I may have ventured into a new way of doing criticism, a form that searches for the birthword, the word-written-on-the-forehead, the bloodword, the rootword, the sunword, the magic word, the boneword, the lifeword, the motherword, the word-stitched-in-the-soul, the fireword. These words are all variations on the spiritword, the word that gives life to literary production.

On days of gloom, I think I've been writing in sand. The wind will blow all my words and names away. Do you have a word that tolls for you? A word you carry or are carried by, a word you hold or are held by, like wind, like water. My wife, Cheryl, has a word. It's the sun. Like a plant, she bends to its light. Do you have a word that stops your bleeding or spells away your gloom? Do you have a word on your lips awaiting utterance?

Living by a word. Hanging by a thread. If you tell me my word, I'll tell you yours. I want to give you my word in this book. I want to give you what I think are the words of others.

I once met a strange man, tall, bizarrely dressed, the clothes of a hunter, capped. He told me that he had his own word, a long word that he had difficulty spelling, a Russian word starting with the letter k. The word was the name of a Russian town, and though he had never been there, he was convinced that the word—and I suppose by extension, the town—belonged to him.

Maybe your word changes as you change. I was often ill as a child. My word then kept changing from pauchle to gerrynose: I was a sickly child with a runny nose. Later I fell in love with the foreign sight and sound of André Malraux's word, *farfelu*: crazy, quixotic adven-

Preface

turer, wild man, person of reckless abandon…Thomas Merton?

Merton's word was mercy, a word to heal his wounds of being alive when his brother was dead, of getting a woman pregnant, of abandoning a son, of finding a woman and then letting her go. Sometimes I think I may have found my word. At other times, I think it is more important to chase after a word than catch it. If I do have a word, I want it to be as ungainly as the capped man's word for a mysterious Russian town.

It's hard to find someone to talk to. Hard and getting harder. Can I find a way of speaking to you that makes you care about Dennis Lee's tremendum and George Grant's obedience? Martin Heidegger's being and Flannery O'Connor's revelation? Raymond Carver's love and Thomas Merton's mercy? I feel like talking the whole night through about strange things. Please listen, though I have no particular right to speak. I'm a little weary, less fit than I would like to be, a little lonely, and sometimes bewildered. "I'm nobody. Who are you?"

These words fall from the lips of Emily Dickinson, that recluse from Amherst whose packets of unpublished poems were found after her death by Irish maids. Forget all the kitsch about Ireland saving civilization. Ireland through these anonymous Irish maids saved a measure of civilization.

Dickinson wasn't really a nobody. She had parents and a brother and a sister and a sister-in-law whom she adored and some minister friends. She read the Bible and Shakespeare and Emerson and some nineteenth-century poets and novelists. She was a reader. She didn't read broadly, but she read deeply. She had a genius for metaphor. She saw double: what was there and what there reminded her of. Everything was always something else while at the same time being fully itself.

Maybe I'm not a nobody either. I have a wife, a son, a daughter, a dog. I'm a reader. A reader, according to B.W. Powe, is "a solitary outlaw." So I'm that too, and a lover of words. I listen for the movement of spirit in the word: its rustle, its crackle. I'm ready now, or as ready as I'll ever be. I launch my nerve. I give you my loves.

I want to talk in the Irish way, in *furrawn*, the talk that leads to intimacy. I want to talk to you about what matters to me most: how words in books sometimes ignite spirit. Or, is it Spirit? I don't know. The spirit is related to Spirit, as beings are related to Being. Sometimes I think I know the difference between the two, and sometimes the difference doesn't matter to me.

Many times I've wanted to talk to you, but I couldn't get the voice right. I can't start talking unless I get the voice right. Voice is everything to me. One false note and I lose you. I don't know how falsity enters into a piece of writing, I don't know how to keep it out, but I hear it when it hisses.

I get this idea of falsity from reading Clarice Lispector, who grew up in Brazil and wrote in Portuguese. I always say to myself: she writes short books because she's afraid of telling a lie in long ones. Every sentence is put under the microscope: is this true? do I

— Preface —

really believe it? have I expressed my doubt and fear and ambivalence sufficiently well? Dennis Lee subjects himself to a similar round of self-criticism.

Please find a way to read this amphibious work, this linguistic place where words and books and spirit meet. I'd like to think that the work in your hands is body-writing, soul-writing, my body to yours, my soul to yours. Do I deceive myself? There's always a danger of pretending to be more than you are or other than you are. I believe with Thoreau that the best you can write is the best you are.

Incidentally, it pleases me that Clarice—she's the sort of writer you call by her first name—read Thoreau and liked him. She read Merton too and liked him. I don't know if she read Dickinson or not. There are no false notes in Dickinson, none. And none in Lispector. These writers put themselves at risk by keeping falsity out, Lispector especially so. She takes things so far out and so deep down that her mental health seems at risk. Can you live without armour? Can you become one with the other and still have a self?

I risk nothing so grandiose here as sanity. But I do put on the table some of the things I love. Suppose you don't love them back. Suppose I haven't convinced you that they are lovable. Suppose I haven't convinced you that I love them sufficiently. You can have a word and not know it. You can have a word and know it. Sometimes you can only see your word when someone else says it for you.

– Spirit Book Word –

Merton knew his word; Grant and Heidegger and Lawrence knew theirs. Lee, I think, knows his. Carver found his word in the last few years of his life. But in the case of Gunnars, O'Connor, Dickinson and Lispector, do they really have the word I ascribe them, or have I merely handed them one of my own words? Perhaps the words you see in others are the words you carry deepest in your own body.

I like to think that the writers in this book all have a word they love with special devotion, a word they have given special urgency. They've found a word by which to animate their literary lives, the way you find your trail by walking it. Each gives her word more body, more spirit, more amplitude than it had before her tongue cut across it. Each finds a word to pour radiance into or draw radiance from.

I
Spirit Book Word

Peter Greenaway's film *The Pillow Book* opens with a father writing the name of his daughter on her forehead and his own name on her chin. That way, he tells her, she will always know who she is. He also tells her a Japanese story. He says, "When God made the first clay model of a human being, He painted in the eyes…and the lips…and the sex… And then He painted in each person's name lest the person should ever forget it…If God approved of His creation, He breathed the painted clay-model into life by signing His own name."

All her life the daughter seeks men with handsome faces and delicate hands to inscribe her body. Later, she inscribes men's bodies and makes literature from their flesh. The first story told to her, then, and the first words written upon her face, have enormous impact. She runs from lover to lover, looking for a word with the power of her first word, looking for a man with the power to write calligraphy as beautiful as her father's.

The poet Basho, so the story goes, wanted to write a final haiku before he died. The haiku named a place he had once visited, Matsushima, a place of bays and islands and "deep green pines shaped by salty winds, trained into sea-wind bonsai." A Japanese friend once told me—apocryphally I'm sure—that as Basho lay dying, he repeated the place name three times with an "ah" punctuating each line. He had moved beyond words and had settled for a sound. The "ah" sounded the note of regret and loss for the painful beauty of passing things. He would never again return to his isle of enchantment, nor would he find a word to re-conjure it.

Some writers, like Basho, seem to have certain words written on their foreheads, and others not. Some writers, like the woman in *The Pillow Book*, seem to have whole scripts written on their bodies.

Shakespeare, despite Ted Hughes' decade-long project to unearth the master metaphor of his language, rattles arms of adjectives, legs of adverbs, thighs of nouns, necks of verbs, whole bodies of words. The man who imaginatively transported his characters all over Europe, to times distant, forgotten or non-existent, commandeered a language as broad as his geography. You could burn every book in the world written in English except his, and still re-spark the language from his embers. He burned from a field of fires.

If Hughes is right that a writer does little else than find metaphors for his own nature, then Shakespeare must have been exceedingly complex. His metaphors

I: Spirit Book Word

sprout in the over-abundance and wild cultivation of an English garden.

For the longest time I felt that I would never find my word, never see it spelt, never be able to use it in a sentence. As an infant, perhaps I was given a word, a word written on my forehead, probably by my father. I lost it in the chaos of living. Is my job somehow to get it back now, decades later, this my birthword?

Words happened to me before books did. Greenaway says the body comes before the book. "'I am old,' said the book. 'I am older,' said the body.'" Words are older than books too, and they course more directly from the body than books do.

Words off the tongue. Words on the stage. Words on the radio. Words in my ear. These were my wordsprings. My word springs. Much later in my childhood I got round to words on the page. There is a common soundstream, though, between the word and the book: voice. Books talk in certain tones as tongues wag in particular ways. Masters of voice and tone, like Thomas Merton and Dennis Lee, have always evoked my strongest allegiance.

I can stand by the words of B.W. Powe in *Outage*, "So much of my life has been spent trying to figure out what others were saying, implying, whispering." I love the sound of my wife's voice, my sister's, my children's. Even the sound of those whom I don't know but often hear: the voices of Alec Guinness, Nora Young, Philippe

Noiret, Martha Henry, William Hutt, John Gielgud, Lily Tomlin, Marlon Brando... I love the sound of Brian Moore, another man from Belfast whom my mother says sounds like my father.

I take to heart Clarissa Estela Estes' words: "Some people are remedied by thunderstorms, some by music, some by the voice of a person they love." I'm voice-broken and voice-mended by those I love.

I remember how the biblical God talks things into being. For me, if salvation comes, it will come in the form of a sound. I wait for the sound. I can't see Spirit, but I can hear It. I'm reminded of a comment Clarice Lispector once made. The only thing material about music is the instrument.

Voices. Sounds. Maybe I heard first the swish of my mother's womb as I bobbed in her sea, or I heard the tick-tock of her heart. I don't know why sounds have such impact on me. The other day I was very happy to come upon Sam Shepard's *Hotel Chronicles and Moon Hawk* and his dog-like sensitivity to sound. I discovered a sound brother. He does for sound in this book what Patrick Suskind did for smell in *Perfume*.

A lexicon of the ear. "The greatest drum solo ever heard was made by a loose flap of a tarpaulin on top of my car hitting the wind at eighty." Shepard is even sensitive to visual sound, the sounds you imagine like "hawk swoops and swan dives." He chronicles an inventory of sound from "saw rhythm" to the "chomp of a horse... Parrots sharpening their beaks on wood. Chickens scratching. Dogs digging... Birds cleaning their feathers..." The earth as a never-silent drum beating out the rhythms of everything that is.

When my father was away at university a good deal during my early childhood, one of the things I missed most was hearing his voice. I missed his goodnight too, and his singing of Irish songs in the car. I missed his reading of scripture at dinner, and his prayers and blessings, and all the good words that would pour from his mouth when he was around. When I read, I listen for voice. Is it his voice I'm still listening for?

Dennis Lee, a poet at play in the wells of sound, has written with authority on the subject of voice. He says "voice embodies a particular timbre of being"; voice gives body to the thing. The first voice I heard, the first "timbre of being," doubtlessly came from my mother.

The mother tongue is often quite literally mother's tongue. My mother stuck her tongue in my ear, and I luxuriated over the strange tickling sounds of her north Irish. From her mouthfuls of articulated air, wind-wafted on her accented voice, I experienced the shock of the strange and the joy of mouthmade words.

Even in Canada, her voice, like winkle to stone, retained remnants of Portavogie in it, and her words, like seashells, always carried me back to the sea, near my stony Irish birthplace. The mothervoice, to this day, seems like a kind of motherland, some acoustic space where I finally feel at home.

I read now for the strangeness and presence of a voice, a way of sounding the world, a way of talking to myself. Writers like Thomas Merton and Kristjana Gunnars have their own way of sounding the world and of talking to themselves. Literature for me must have a strange, spoken presence—as strange as Clarice Lispector. As strange as the Gospels. As strange as the Penguin Café Orchestra making warm-up noises till the noises turn to music as water once turned to wine.

Dennis Lee talks authoritatively about sound and voice in his *Body Music*. "Most of my life," he says, "is spent listening into a cadence which is a kind of taut cascade, a luminous tumble… I take my vocation to consist of listening in this cadence…listening into it with enough life concentration that it can become words through me if it chooses."

Lee articulates the sound-ground from which his own music pipes as a mishmash of "raunchy saxophone" and "vibrant cello." (While composing *Riffs* he listened to Bach's "Unaccompanied Cello Suites" and Little Walter's blues.) The organ and the flute sometimes chime in too. As a poet, he hears sounds, and he bodies them back in words.

"First Poets, then the Sun," says Emily Dickinson in one of her ecstatic moods, in one of her exuberant sounds. There are days when I believe her. The sun is the sun, after all, a burning disc in the sky. For it to be more than that requires poetry.

Experiencing the sun William Blake experienced— angels and fiery chariots—requires poetry. To imagi-

I: Spirit Book Word

natively drape the sun, in the manner of the wrap artist Christo, or to strip it bare, in the manner of a Samuel Beckett, requires poetry, maximalist or minimalist.

On some days poets do rank higher than suns. For the necessary humanization of the Foreign and the personalization of the Other, great pulleys of poetry are required to hoist what is out there in here and jet our hearts to distant spinning stars.

In my early days, poets certainly came before the sun.

After emigrating from Ireland with my family when I was four, we settled into Esterhazy, Saskatchewan, a potash mining town. We didn't stay long, just long enough for frigid weather and the Northern Lights. A year or two later, we moved to another mining town, Cardiff in Ontario, famous for uranium deposits and the ubiquitous blackfly. Dad was a United Church minister, not fully licensed, so we travelled like Gypsies to where we were called. My sister Caroline went through something like eleven schools in fifteen years. My own knocking about was less drastic.

When I was about eight, Dad took me to Stratford to hear the supreme poet of our language. Perhaps not altogether consciously, he stumbled upon an art form that fused his love of history, biography and poetry: Shakespeare's histories. First came Henry VIII and then most of the other history plays, followed by a smattering of the comedies and the tragedies.

I loved the sword-fighting, the costumes and the strange speech of Kings and ale-drinkers. In comparison with everyday speech, which seemed so feckless and moribund, Shakespeare whooshed like a suddenly lit fire. You got the gist of things even if the specifics eluded you.

Once you've had an early snort of Shakespeare, your sensorium is never the same again. Your ear, like a sponge holding water, retains traces of distant gurgles. I still use sound to make my judgements about truthfulness: "This sounds right. That sounds wrong." Even judgements about people: "She sounds good. I like the sound of him."

From Shakespeare, Dad handed me over to the Romantic poets. He placed me in the care of visionaries like Blake, Wordsworth and Keats. He played records of English actors with pleasing voices reading from the poets' visionary works. He physically took me where the poets of the English Lake District had walked over fern-covered hills and talked as they walked so I could say years later: "Yes, I once trod where great poets had trodden." He took me to Yeats' Country in Sligo, so I could touch the poet's stone-tower and count his swans at Coole.

I continue to get excited when I trip on a poem, or a poet, I haven't listened to before. For instance, Anne Carson and her "god poems." My most joyous state in reading is to taste the ripe words of a good poem on my tongue. A few days ago, I read for the first time Galway Kinnell's "Blackberry Eating," one of the New York City subway poems. The poem takes an unexpected turn from berry to word, from blackberry-eating to language-making.

At the precise moment of the turn, I shook with rapture: "...the ripest berries/fall almost unbidden to my tongue,/as words sometimes do..." There it is; there's the moment: "as words sometimes do"... Kinnell extends the analogy: "many-lettered, one-syllabled lumps,/which I squeeze, squinch open, and splurge well/ in the silent, startled, icy, black language/of blackberry-eating in late September."

Why do I read poetry? Quite simply, for sounds like "silent, startled, icy, black language," and magical fusions of the world's body parts. I read it for liftoff, those times when words induce levitation or flight, when the language is unbearably beautiful, like sunlight in my wife's hair. I read it for the swoosh of Ur-sound, the vibration that makes all things tremble. I read it for moments of transfixion, moments comparable to listening to the music of Jan Garbarek's saxophone or Keith Jarrett's piano.

So words traipsed into my life before books did. The Shakespearean whoosh before anything else. Words in thunder and in lightning. Soundstorms. The book and I made a comparatively late acquaintance. Long before we met, Mom's recitation of Yeats' "Lake Isle of Innisfree" and Dad's Shakespeare had already lined my ears with a hunger for more and different sounds. The new sounds jingled by way of the book.

I was in grade eight. Bored. Often falling asleep in class. One morning my dove-haired math teacher, Mr. Karpiak, walked in and began reading the first lines of Victor Hugo's *Les Misérables*. He took a whole year to get through it. I knew his secret.

He knew that the only way to get some of us to school, and once there to keep us awake, was to read four or five pages a day from Hugo, leaving off just when we begged him to go on. *Les Misérables*, "Les Miz" in musical prattle, marked the beginning of my awakening into the world of books.

Here I deliberately deploy the Buddha's master metaphor of sleep and wakefulness, for so much of the human journey, and in particular my own slow development, has had to do with movement from somnolence to a measure of wakefulness.

I am a sleepy Proustian being, and in Hugo I awoke to the novel, to literature and to the counterlife of the imagination, as earlier I had awoken to the strange sounds of Shakespeare. I've never forgotten Jean Valjean's stolen loaf or the detective Javert's unjust pursuit of a good man.

You seldom forget the spells of your first enchantment. My son, Daniel, has never forgotten Dr. Seuss, nor my daughter, Rachel, Arnold Lobel, by whose rhythms she learned to read.

My spells came through my ear. First Shakespeare and the poets. Then Victor Hugo. With Shakespeare I was never conscious that his words were housed in a book—rather, they were out in the wilds, on the winds—whereas, with Hugo, I had a sense that his words fell from a book. No doubt this sense partly derived from the fact that my teacher held the book in his hand as he read.

The first book I read on my own was probably Jack London's *Call of the Wild*; it was an early read of Clarice Lispector's too. I was reading Classic Comics at the time. Comics along with sports stories and dog stories. Getting a taste of what I would come back to later and read unabridged.

London made his dogs into heroes, and I remember thinking how I would like to be brave and overcome hardship the way Buck does in the novel. The literary dog was perhaps the first character I fully identified with in fiction. And to this day, I enjoy reading the novelist Milan Kundera for many reasons, not the least of which is his loving portraits of dogs.

A confession: George Grant and Emily Dickinson are dear to me in part because of their excessive love of Arthur and Carlo, their respective dogs. Dickinson has a line somewhere, "Go tell Carlo and he'll tell me," sweeter than honey. Kristjana Gunnars has a German shepherd in the back of her narrator's pick-up truck in *The Substance of Forgetting*. In the same novel she borrows my mother's "Innisfree" as bookends. That's what I remember best about her novel: the poem and the dog.

After Jack London in my early teens came *Prester John* and *The Catcher in the Rye*. Then Hemingway, some D.H. Lawrence essays, poems and stories, the plays of Arthur Miller and the pornography of Henry Miller, some Mailer, some Hesse and a great deal of Jonathan Swift. Orwell and Camus, too. These writers lived on my street, just up the road or just around the corner.

I remember writers the way some remember love affairs. I remember the genealogy of my reading the way the Bible remembers who begets whom. Shouldn't there be a biblical injunction to impel a lifelong affair with words in books? I remember all the days of my reading and all the books in my life. Bookscapes better than landscapes.

I remember reading Melville in the back seat of my uncle's car en route to Montreal, bethundered by his Shakespearean speech. I remember a summer of Milan Kundera, a summer of Raymond Carver, then more recently, summers of Kristjana Gunnars and Clarice Lispector. I remember a decade and more with the poet-monk Thomas Merton. What would I remember if I couldn't remember books?

There's a painting in the Art Gallery of Hamilton by George Reid of a young boy in a hayloft, reading. Head in hand, a cap on his head, shadows falling. In my imagination, that's me, reading and dreaming, reading in dreamtime, in amongst the hay...oblivious to my mother's call to supper.

The Hungarian photographer André Kertèsz presents a book which consists solely of images of people reading. He gives the reader Vermeer-like attention. He photographs the human family at book: young and

I: Spirit Book Word

old, fat and thin, rich and poor, in myriad locations, including an old woman lying on a canopied bed with a book in her wrinkled hands. My heart quickens. I look at these photographs as if I'm looking at prayerful monks, as if I've stumbled into the Matisse chapel in Vence or the Rothko prayer room in Houston.

Some days all I want to do is read, read one good book well, with love and discernment, scratch a few words out about it, and that would be sufficient, a full enough life. Reading, to borrow Raymond Carver's beautiful phrase, is "a small, good thing." Books are small, good things. I want to take the book to heart, play it on the heartstrings and introduce it to the hungry soul. I want to read dreamily, bodily, nomadically, dialogically, meditatively, naturally... Reading as natural to my body as a sigh. I want to read for what D.H. Lawrence wrote for: "the real flame of feeling," "the shimmering protoplasm," and "life wild at the source."

I come to a book shyly, as I would to a temple. I open it as I would a snake-basket. I'm not sure of the exact nature of the reptile, but I know it might be dangerous, even lethal. I wait expectantly, patiently, for the bite. I pray that it may be life-altering.

During the bite or during the time in which I wait for it, I remember the words of Proust: "Reading is at the threshold of spiritual life; it can introduce [you] to it," but "it does not constitute it."

In May, 1965—I was fourteen at the time—Dad gave me Dietrich Bonhoeffer's *Letters & Papers from Prison*: in Ezra Pound's phrase, one of the world's "balls of light." He inscribed these words: "May his courage be yours. In right and in wrong." His book-gift signalled my theological coming of age. I was now able, in his mind, to read important European theologians like Paul Tillich and Dietrich Bonhoeffer. I knew otherwise. I wasn't ready for Bonhoeffer (or Tillich, for that matter) when he was given to me, but it moved me to think that my father thought I was ready.

In many ways, I'm still not ready for Bonhoeffer. You grow into his work, slowly—words take on excruciating gravity when you're about to die—and perhaps you never occupy it completely. From this father-to-son gift, I came away thinking that words and books were strong spiritual forces for good in the world. They could help you live more, feel more, be more.

But I still hadn't found my word. The word that called me, claimed me, owned me. The word written on my body. The word that branded itself in my forehead the way "Being" burnt itself into Heidegger, the way love surrounded Carver or the way "modernism" scalded Swift. I hadn't found a way to link my Trinity: words, books and spirit. I knew vaguely that the words I was primarily interested in revealed themselves (hid themselves?) in books, and I knew what little I understood of spirit had derived from my readings. But I hadn't consciously linked the three in wordlock.

I: Spirit Book Word

I still, in the words of the U2 song, hadn't "found what I was looking for." I hadn't learned to read for spirit, for the spirit-in-the-word. Or, is it the Spirit-in-the-Word?

Marilyn Gear Pilling, a poet and friend in Hamilton, suggested that the "word" itself was my word. For a time I thought I would call this word-hunt, this book-raid, this spirit-chase, *The Book of Words*. I'd been charmed by *The Pillow Book* (novel, movie and movie script) and *The Book of Questions* by Edmond Jabès. But *The Book of Words* was a little too close to *Hamlet*, and the "word" was at once too broad and too narrow. It took in everything but clasped nothing.

Then, one day I found myself in my favourite Toronto bookshop, Pages, on Queen Street. I was with the sculptor Ted Rettig. We both grazed on new offerings. I picked up a Paul Celan in a new translation, the one by Pierre Joris: German on the one side, English on the other.

I read words like "breathturn," "woundmirror," "wellchants," "wordspoor," "firethoughts," "wordblood," "woodsong," "wordmembraned"…with amazement, with my tongue hanging out. Some of the compounds worked for me, others didn't. Sometimes I'd ask Ted about the German originals.

Later a line from George Grant came to mind. "How does one translate properly this polysyllabic language of compounds [German] into a language which has reached its greatest heights in the use of the monosyllable [English]?"

In Pages, at the first moment of recognition, what struck me was a sequence of grunts and gropings... "wordspiritbook," "bookspiritword," "spiritwordbook" ...and finally "spiritbookword." This was the compound that worked for me. First, spirit from the Latin *spiritus*: breathing, breath, air, life, soul. In my personal translation: breath-voice, voiced breath. Then the bridge between spirit and word, in the form of the book. And lastly the word itself: that which is formed in the book and moulded by the spirit. Spiritbookword: the breath of the word in the book.

I jumped up and down like a four-year-old. Hallelujah! I had found my word. I could now look for spiritbookwords in others.

II
Love

Cheryl thinks we should just get in the car one lollapalooza afternoon and drive out to Carver country, Raymond Carver and Tess Gallagher country, Port Angeles in Washington State. We should phone up Tess and tell her we like her poems and we like her husband's stories, and how about a coffee, or would you mind if we dropped in just to see what furniture you have and see that painting of salmon leaping upstream by your friend Alfredo Arreguin called "The Hero's Journey." Some days Cheryl and I live by Carver, the tall man with the soft voice, the way Carver and Gallagher lived by Chekhov in their last months together. His life has interpenetrated ours, a stone we turn to when we're in trouble.

Lately, we've taken to reading Carver to each other in bed, a kind of nightcap. We take turns reading "A Small, Good Thing" aloud, our voices only holding up for a page or two before we pass the story to the other. If you've read any Carver at all, you've probably read this one. It's as good as anything in Flannery O'Connor, though much more tolerant of human frailty.

A father and mother are at the hospital waiting for the word on their dying son, who has been hit by a car. It's the son's birthday, and they've ordered a cake from a baker. The phone keeps ringing. A voice says the cake is ready, and wants to know when they're going to pick it up and pay for it. The phone keeps ringing, and the voice gets more and more menacing. The couple fret over whose voice is calling, determine it's the baker, and drive out to see him. They want to kill him. But instead, he serves them freshly baked cinnamon rolls, and they listen to his story.

The miracle of food in Carver. You witness it in "Cathedral" where the meal begins to turn the husband around. You see it in "A Small, Good Thing" where the baker bakes and the aggrieved couple begin to accept their son's death and forgive the baker's untimely calls. You see it in "Fever" where Mrs. Webster, baking with and for the kids, spoonfeeds the husband through his fever. "Now I'm going to feed this cereal to you. And you're going to open up and eat it. Six bites, that's all. Here, here's the first bite."

Food brings people together in Carver just as alcohol drives them apart. After Carver, I don't want to read a story collection anymore that doesn't tell me what's being served at the table. The table in Carver has a kind of New Testament resonance. Small miracles happen. Take "Feathers," for example. The peacock and the ugly baby story.

A city couple visits a country couple, reluctantly. The country couple are cornball hicks, their house garishly decorated, with a peacock incongruously plunked in the front yard, and they have the ghastliest baby anybody has ever seen. The city couple, particularly the wife, regard themselves as sophisticated. The baby begins to cry and won't stop. The mother brings the baby to the table; they take turns holding it, but it still won't stop crying. They eat ham, mashed potatoes and sweet corn, but the baby won't stop. The country husband asks his wife to bring the peacock in; his wife at first refuses but finally relents, and in struts the peacock. The baby stops crying.

As everyone tucks into the supper, slowly things start to change. Love spills across the room, and the visiting man makes a wish that whatever happens in his life he won't forget the peacock at the table. He knows the transformation won't last; things will snap back. Shortly after the visit, his wife has a baby, gets fat, they argue, they don't see the country couple anymore, but he remembers a baby playing with a peacock at the dinner table.

I only want to write if I'm in love. But can you be in love and write about being in love at the same time? And isn't all love, as Jonathan Swift suggests, self-love anyway, loving our own face in someone else's? I wouldn't want to write about Carver if I weren't in love with his work, in love with the image I have of him and Tess Gallagher, and in love with Cheryl who shares my interest in his life and work. There's something Pauline and wonderful about somebody who's asked if he feels more at home in the house in Washington State or in the house in Syracuse, where he's teaching, and he answers: "No, wherever I am is fine. This is fine."

I like Carver's guilelessness. I like his astonishment at being alive. I like his female characters—sexy, sassy and strong. I like his capacity for change; he was always finding new paths to the waterfall. I like Cheryl's memory of biographical detail, about how Tess would keep his writing going by telling him he hadn't reached Coleman's yet, a place they liked to eat at. She'd tell him the work wasn't worthy of such a good Irish pub; a hamburger joint would have to do. Then when the work got as strong as it could get, she'd tell him they had arrived at Coleman's now. I like how his last prose work is entitled "Meditation On A Line From Saint Teresa" in which he quotes the Saint herself: "Words lead to deeds…They prepare the soul, make it ready, and move it to tenderness."

Good writing comes from Venus or Mars, don't you think, the resident deities of scribblers, or scops as they were once called in Ireland. You make love or you make war. Flannery O'Connor made war. Clarice Lispector made love. I usually prefer the shrine of Venus, though Swift's scorpion sting and Voltaire's martial arts certainly appeal to my intemperate Irish blood. Anyway, love is the only state of being in which I can write or would want to write. Who would want to write without love for the day's light, his wife's funky voice or the unselfconsciousness of dogs? I wouldn't want to write about Raymond Carver's work unless I thought that one

— II: Love —

of his stories or poems could, like a good wind, turn me around.

What Carver objected to in literary criticism was savagery and small-mindedness, the lack of love. I recall his objection to a Hemingway biography: the biographer had chosen to write about someone he loathed. Carver couldn't understand that, how anyone would choose a subject for which he felt neither respect nor affection. You should only write about the things and the people you love. This was a creed Carver lived by, although he would have understood Roland Barthes' words too: you always fail in writing about the things you love.

Cheryl likes to say that I live by fiction, by poetry. Certainly my mood goes up if, on a given day, I read a good story or a good poem; and down, if I fail to. "You haven't had somebody under your skin like this for a long time," she tells me, "not since Merton." Well, Carver is even creeping into my Merton. For the last few years I've conducted a weekend workshop at Five Oaks in Paris, Ontario, on Tom Merton's life. Last year I used Carver's story "Cathedral." This year I plan to use "Fat," the baker poem, maybe "A Small, Good Thing," likely "Feathers" and maybe even "The Compartment."

Some of Carver's stories are bleak, particularly "The Compartment," but when the dark is seen clearly and swallowed completely, it loses its spookiness, perhaps.

Carver gathered his best in the new and selected stories he called *Where I'm Calling From*, but I wish he hadn't left out "The Compartment." For that one you need to visit the *Cathedral* collection, his most integrated gathering, every story a star in the firmament. "The Compartment" concerns a father on a train setting out to see his son, whom he hasn't seen in eight years. But after losing the watch he bought for his son, he can't bring himself to get off the train. He rides on, not in majesty, but in resignation.

I can't live by Carver for as long as I've lived by Merton. There are too few works. Not like my monk with his legions of books. I can read Merton for the rest of my life and still not come to the end of him. Whereas, with Carver, you can carry his storybooks in one hand and his poetry in the other, and one or two mixed volumes in your teeth. You can carry his soul in *Where I'm Calling From*, 526 pages of some of the best short fiction since Anton Chekhov, the one who occupied a place of honour on Carver's study wall.

You want to have Carver's stories by your bedside in the same way you want Rilke's poems and Van Gogh's letters, amulets, stones to finger in a storm. You want to give the book to friends, the way the actor Rod Steiger liked to pass out copies of *The Little Prince* to strangers.

How I got started on Carver was through my friend Mark Garber, who passed along "Errand" from an old

II: Love

New Yorker. I couldn't get into it at the time. I put it down. Then a few weeks later another friend, Wayne Allan, passed along "Cathedral." I started to read it and couldn't stop, the story of an angry and isolated husband who's jealous of his wife's blind friend coming for dinner. The husband manages to keep quiet during the meal—everyone gives eating his full attention—and slowly civility replaces bad manners. After a few scotches and a couple of joints—Carver's characters eat, drink and smoke prodigiously—the husband's wife falls asleep, leaving the two men to get along on their own.

The husband clicks on the television, finds nothing suitable, and finally settles on a program on the building of cathedrals. The husband doesn't know much more about cathedrals than the blind man, but in the process of trying to describe them, and failing, he confesses his inadequacy. The blind man asks the husband if he is religious. He says he isn't; he says he doesn't believe in cathedrals or in anything else; he says it's hard sometimes. Finally, in exasperation, the husband says about cathedrals that "they're something to look at on late-night TV." That's all.

The blind man suddenly asks the husband to get paper and pencil and draw a cathedral. The husband, unexpectedly, carries out the request. As he draws, the blind man places his hand over the husband's and somehow senses that the husband hasn't put any people in the cathedral. He reminds the husband that you can't have a cathedral without people. Then he asks the husband to close his eyes. At this point, two blind men begin to see. "Cathedral" is a story in which a blind man teaches a sighted man to see.

I read somewhere that in Buenos Aires there's a bookshop that also serves coffee and sandwiches. The bookshop-restaurant serves a salad called "Carver" and a sandwich called "Cathedral." So Carver's on a restaurant menu in Argentina! The "Cathedral Sandwich" consists of cheese and lettuce on white bread—the simplest things. The story too consists of the simplest things: a husband, a wife, a blind man, in triangular tension. It's one of Carver's lightning stories. "Writing is trouble," Carver says, "but once in a great while lightning strikes." But the lightning doesn't strike those for whom writing isn't "very nearly the most important thing in their lives, right up there next to breath, and food, and shelter, and love, and God."

If you haven't read "Cathedral," read it. It's one of those transformation stories Carver is so good at, a story in which he moves from Hemingway's sparseness to Chekhov's richer, fuller idiom, a watershed work. Apparently, he woke up one morning after a good night's sleep—Carver belongs to the fraternity of insomniacs—sat down at his desk and "something happened," he says. "I knew it was a different kind of story for me... Somehow I had found another direction I wanted to move toward. And I moved. And quickly."

I shook with fear the first time I read the story, damn this is good, it's too good, how can something be this good. Then I went back to "Errand," a story about the death of Chekhov and his doctor's ordering of champagne, and then went from story to story the way a child jumps from one stone to another in crossing a creek.

Raymond Carver has been called a minimalist by John Updike. The British magazine *Granta* has depicted him as a practitioner of dirty realism; he's also been called a neo-realist, and a writer of K-mart fiction. He never bought into the labels, particularly minimalist. But he is a minimalist if being one means saying big things with little words or saying many things with few words; he's not, if it means writing with pinched emotion. Carver's people, which is the word Carver gives to his fictional characters, give life everything they've got, although what they have to give often isn't enough.

Carver writes about waitresses, apartment caretakers, vacuum cleaner salesmen, vitamin sellers, heavy drinkers and junk-food eaters, fishermen, guilt-ridden husbands, factory workers, postmen, mechanics and bakers. His people are often out of work or can't pay the rent, live in terror of the telephone, can't fall asleep (see "The Student's Wife" on the pains of sleeplessness, akin to Hemingway's "Now I Lay Me"), or fight to stay sober. He writes about sons estranged from their fathers, husbands estranged from their wives; he writes about drinking and bickering, and worry; he writes about breakups and breakdowns and excess.

He has written some of the best booze stories around, as good as John Cheever's, though nothing quite as funny as Cheever's father-and-son Beefeater gin story. He takes you inside a detox centre ("Where I'm Calling From"), inside the gauzy speech alcohol induces ("What We Talk About When We Talk About Love"), and inside the fight to remain sober ("Chef's House").

Carver respects work in his stories and poems. In his tribute to John Gardner in "Work" the speaker concludes, "And work/Yes, work/The going/to what lasts." He lives by the code of Ecclesiastes: whatever your right hand finds to do, do it with your might. In "The Juggler At Heaven's Gate" the speaker extols "But to juggle/for God's sake/To give your life to that/To go with that/Juggling," and in "After Rainy Days" the speaker spots a man struggling to reel in a salmon below a footbridge and thinks, "Stay with him.../For Christ's sake, man, hold on!" Work is whatever you're doing and trying to do well.

People are hanging on in a good Carver story, getting by the best they can. Sometimes, as in "Cathedral," they're open to love and sometimes they're susceptible to violence, as in "What We Talk About When We Talk About Love," where tension slowly gives way to terror. Sometimes menace, like an overhead fan heard but not seen, beats its invisible wings. You finish some of the stories and you say to yourself, "Where's this going to go? Somebody's going to get hurt here."

In "Chef's House" everything comes out taut, the feelings corked. The narrator holds the words back like a man trying to stand upright in a fast current. You know he can't hold out, or hold off what's coming. He's going to be overwhelmed, he's going to drown, but in a moment of stasis, just as long as the story lasts, there's "a momentary stay against confusion." You read this story and you want to burst. You know a gun is going to go off. This story, like many of Carver's, has what Richard Ford calls the "illusion—that this is about as close as language can come to representing actuality." The story also brings to mind a line from the Carver-Gallagher screenplay *Dostoevsky*, "One must simply restrain oneself at every moment, no matter what the heat of the game."

Where did this master of capped tension come from? Cheryl and I ask ourselves. How did he get to be who he became? His father, a saw-filer in a sawmill; his mother, by turns, a waitress, a retail clerk, a housewife. No one in the family goes beyond grade school. In the early years Carver lives in two-bedroom houses, shares a room with his brother, uses an outdoor toilet, has no car, and by age twenty is married with two children. To get by, he pumps gas, picks tulips, sweeps hospital corridors, swabs toilets and manages an apartment complex. He travels a long way from a home that doesn't seem capable of turning out a writer of his stature. He overcomes hurdle and hoop, including the alcoholism that by 1977 had almost killed him, in order to have some quiet and privacy to write sentences.

He does get some help along the way. As a delivery boy for a pharmacist, he wanders into an elderly man's home that has books and poetry magazines lying about.

The man expresses the hope that Carver might one day write for the magazines he sees on the coffee table. He gets help from his teacher John Gardner who gives him a key to his office so Carver has a quiet place to do his writing. He also gets help from his first wife, Maryann, who introduces him to good literature. The early books are dedicated to her.

After *Cathedral*, everything is dedicated to Tess, and in the last work, *The New Path to the Waterfall*, Carver incantationally writes "Tess. Tess. Tess. Tess," one of the loveliest dedications in the language. There's little doubt, though, that Maryann held him up in the alcohol years, a debt Carver was keenly aware of.

In "Intimacy" Carver recreates a situation in which a writer returns to his wife to ask forgiveness for using their lives as story fodder. Lines in the story echo from Maryann's separation from Carver, lines like "For the longest time I was inconsolable," and "After that time, when you went away, nothing much mattered after that." A friend of Carver's once said that Ray and Maryann paid for the stories with their lives. Certainly she appears to have paid for them with hers.

In a 1991 interview published in *...when we talk about Raymond Carver*, she seems wobbly, resentful at the playing down of her influence on Carver's writing, shaky on the question of her identity apart from her role as an early Carver catalyst. Her love for him scorches the interview pages. Carver was one of those rare souls, loved deeply not by one woman but by two.

– II: Love –

Maybe because Carver had a hard go of it in childhood, at work, with alcohol, and in his first marriage, he knew what it was like to be submerged, and have to struggle from under something. He calls his characters submerged, and you can see the word made flesh in the bellhop in "Errand" who is awestruck by Chekhov. You can see it too in "The Baker" poem in which Pancho Villa introduces the baker's wife as his girlfriend to Count Vronsky. After talking about women and horses, Pancho falls asleep. The baker crosses himself and leaves the house.

He's going to run away and save his life because he's in a situation he can't handle, and he seems to know the AA gospel of distinguishing between things you can change and things you can't. Carver writes, "That anonymous husband, barefooted,/humiliated, trying to save his life, he/is the hero of this poem."

You wonder, by the way, if this poem baker is an ancestor of the short story baker in "A Small, Good Thing." In Carver sometimes his story-poems beget short stories. The poem "Distress Sale" leads to the story "Why Don't You Dance?", one of Carver's funniest about a man selling in his driveway everything he owns. The poem "Late Night with Fog and Horses" leads to "Blackbird Pie" and "Mother" leads to "Boxes" and so on. Sometimes what he first casts in poetic miniature he recasts in full story later.

On Cheryl's suggestion, I plan to put Carver on my college literature courses in the fall. I want to take slides of the faces in Bob Adelman's *Carver Country*: of the blind man, of Ray, of Tess, of Carver's birthplace in Oregon, his desk (above it a picture of Chekhov), a plaster cast of Tess's teeth which he uses in "Feathers," his family, and friends, like Richard Ford. I want the students to feel that this guy is real, that his fictional world is the real thing. They get fed so many lies. Maybe Carver's honesty will be refreshing, and the Pound dictum he lived by: "Fundamental accuracy of statement is the ONE sole morality of writing."

One good thing I can do for my students is give them Yevtushenko's "Lies" and some Carver stories, so they can see that honesty is still possible in a world of slogans and snow-jobs. I want them to say to themselves, quietly: this guy started small and grew; maybe I can grow too. I want them to feel the love of language that Carver puts into every word, the love of things, everyday objects, and the love he had for Tess and Tess for him so that they say to themselves, quietly: maybe I could love like that; maybe someone could love me.

It's the love story, finally, we're suckers for, isn't it? Maryann risks everything for love and loses; Tess risks everything and wins, for a time. You never win with love for long. Betrayal or self-delusion or death always enters in. And somehow you know that whatever happens to you, you're going to grow into that word in Marguerite Duras' novel about lovers—ravaged. You're going to be ravaged by love, the only thing worth being ravaged by. Ever since "Dover Beach" we've known that in a post-everything time we need love above all. Someone to kiss and be kissed by. And what a love story the Carver-Gallagher saga is.

They finish Carver's *A New Path to the Waterfall* together under the death-threat of lung cancer, reading Chekhov to each other, going to Reno to get married and for a little Dostoevskian gambling, Ray's face and shaved head looking more and more like the Buddha's. Do Cheryl and I like underdogs, folks who roll the dice defiantly, lovers who don't quit? You bet. So we celebrate David and Jonathan, Naomi and Ruth, Gatsby and Daisy, Jake and Brett, Desdemona and Othello, Antony and Cleopatra ("Whole empires are shattered as [they] rush into each other's arms"), Carver and Gallagher. And maybe some day we'll go back to Lady Gregory's estate in Sligo and carve our initials and Ray's and Tess's into Yeats' big tree.

I'm always interested in what people say and think when they knowingly approach their end. Carver knew he was coming to the end, knew in his heart that Mark Strand line, "in/A world without Heaven all is farewell." By 1987 he had a year or so to write, to get down last things. And at the end he's still writing his signature terror fiction where small things take on terrifying significance, where a small turn in luck spells disaster. The fragility of goodness. The fragility of love. That's what Carver is writing in terror of at the end: fragilities and the terror of losing them, fragilities and the terror of their breaking; how an obsession about bass ("The Third Thing That Killed My Father") can destroy a man or an unsaid word ("Blackbird Pie") can bring down a marriage, or a glass of champagne ("Errand") can consummate a life.

"Errand," his last story, uses the basic storyline of Henri Troyat's biography, *Chekhov*. What's interesting is not so much what Carver borrows from the biography—Tolstoy's visit, a loyal and caring wife, a good doctor, Chekhov's insouciance—but what he adds to it. He adds a bellhop who doesn't quite know what to make of a dying man drinking champagne. You have the feeling that he won't be quite the same again, and you remember the rightness of Tobias Wolff's remark, "His life is illuminated by something he cannot fathom."

At the end, Carver is making lists, as Chekhov was once reading schedules of the trains running out of Moscow before he died. He writes on a scrap of paper: "eggs, peanut butter, hot choc, Australia? Antarctica?" He has dreams of going to Russia, and of standing by Chekhov's grave. He writes the best poems of his career, poems of immense gratitude, like "Gravy."

> No other word will do…
>
> Gravy, these past ten years.
>
> Alive, sober, working, loving and
>
> being loved by a good woman…
>
> "I'm a lucky man.

II: Love

I've had ten years longer than I or anyone

expected. Pure gravy. And don't forget it."

He writes a poem about Tess and three kisses, which Cheryl and I try to get through and can't. And he writes a farewell, an exquisite poem of parting, called "Late Fragment," which closes *A New Path to the Waterfall*.

And did you get what

you wanted from this life, even so?

I did.

And what did you want?

To call myself beloved, to feel myself

beloved on the earth.

Love is the final breath in Raymond Carver's life, and in his work.

III
Small

Kristjana Gunnars, like Raymond Carver, is a writer of small books. A maker of microcosmos. A maker of small, good things. Each new book seems smaller and thinner than the last. Fewer pages, fewer words. More space, more silence. You ask yourself: "How far will she go? Will she eventually disappear?" Her book, a non-book; her writing, non-writing; her body of words as slight as a Giacometti sculpture.

"I want my stories to be small," she says in a poem. Her books fit in your hand. They're tiny and thin. Her books, like Raymond Carver's and Clarice Lispector's, concern little things: moods and shifts in perception. Gunnars reads and then she writes. She often writes about what she reads.

In *The Rose Garden* she reads and writes about Marcel Proust and a handful of other writers. She "read-writes"—shouldn't there be a Germanic compound yoking the two oxen to one cart?—a garden, a small German town, her lover and herself, and maybe, through her satchel of writers, the world at large.

Spirit Book Word

She inhales the worlds around her like scents in a garden. She breathes the world in and then out in soft moods and gentle tones: a misty Turner crossed with a "thingy" Vermeer, a moody violin alongside the clarity of a trumpet.

You don't so much read her as soak in her, bathing in her voices and moods. After a good soaking, you say to yourself, "Something small and strange has come into the world. Something different."

Gunnars' world is book-lined, sentence-scaffolded, word-joisted. She's made of words. Lost-and-found words, saved words, missing words, trembling words, pristine words, words of desire, words of anguish, words of wish. Her identity seems slight at times. Word-logged. The "I" of her *Rose Garden* sometimes gets lost in the stacks. Book-bound. "Who am I?" she silently poses.

In *The Rose Garden* Gunnars' reading self dominates her writing self. As Daphne Marlatt once remarked, to write is "to tear, to cut, to incise." On the other hand, to read is "to fit together." In *The Rose Garden* Gunnars fits many things together: thoughts with sensations, theories with moods, concepts with settings. She fits writing and reading together too, as if her reading mended the holes her writing made. She joins one writer to another and another, until her Great Chain of Being becomes a great chain of literary beings.

– III: Small –

Her ring is authentic. Her style is clean and spare.

It's easier to say what kind of reader Gunnars is than to say what kind of writer she is. She reads closely, carefully, connectively, leapingly. She wants you to read too. She includes a bibliography at the end of the book. She writes poems and stories and novels, and what you might call unclassifiable books. These I like best. The unclassifiable ones, more a library than a particular section in the library. Part memoir, part meditational essay, part narrative, part reflective reading. She writes intimately, economically, imagistically, moodily.

Her *Rose Garden* dissolves the Many into the One and disperses the One into the Many. Gunnars thinks and feels centrifugally and centripetally. Her book cross-pollinates the way journals sometimes do, or the way love letters try to. It's a book I wish I had written, one's own body melding into other bodies, a mix of fact and fantasy.

The book combines clarity and mystery, embrace and penetration, mood and desire. It's at once scholarly and sensuous. Its prose technique reminds me a little of Peter Dale Scott's poetry where poem and commentary share a common space. The self is extended through its grounding in others and its reach for others.

Gunnars in *The Rose Garden* chimes all her divergent voices into a single music. A pleasant sadness, an evaporating joy. She writes the way Vermeer's "Maid with the Milk Jug" pours: with strong hands and rapt attention. She's awake, alert, attentive in her narrative-descriptive-meditation. The poet and the storyteller braid with the philosopher, a little Yasunari Kawabata knit into a little Martin Heidegger?

The book I'm holding in my hand takes place in a German rose garden. In the garden, Kristjana Gunnars (or, a voice Gunnars chooses to use) is reading Proust. I too once read Proust languidly in a garden, not of roses, but of jacaranda and bougainvillea, on Makoma Road, a few miles from Victoria Falls, with monkeys in the trees and hippos you had to dodge on your way to your river-nightcap beneath the spilt-gold sunsets on the Zambezi. You always remember when a writer of Proust's stature falls into your lap, just as you remember a bull elephant with a broken tusk, standing motionless on a hill, at sunset.

The author whose book I'm holding in my hands is two years older than I am. She comes originally from Iceland, Reykjavik to my Belfast, from snow and sleet instead of my birthright rain; she looks sad, a sad-eyed lady of the snowlands. Ireland and Iceland, rain and snow, ire and ice. The two countries are linked in my imagination, not least because the Irish poet Louis MacNeice wrote poems about each.

Gunnars is a poet and a storyteller, a reader and a meditator on what she reads, a language tracer and caresser. Her *Rose Garden* is the size of an outstretched hand; all her books seem to fit comfortably in your hand. They feel like home.

– III: Small –

Of late I've started to think about the places, mental and physical, where I feel at home. Most of the time I don't feel at home, so it doesn't surprise me that I would want to count the times and the places when I do. Books generally feel like home to me; they're a kind of homeland, in George Steiner's inspired wording.

I've started to think about why certain images and sounds and books are satisfying to me. Why I feel as if I'm being called home when I see or hear or read certain things. At the moment I'm reading Kristjana Gunnars' *The Rose Garden: Reading Marcel Proust* and feeling very satisfied.

A satisfying book for me seems to have something to do with size. When you read *Gulliver's Travels*, you realize how size charges everything, changes everything. I used to think the perfect book size was something like a hundred pages, a little more, a little less. The size of Camus' *Stranger* or his *Fall*, the size of John Berger's *And our faces, my heart, brief as photos*. Short, almost perfect, books feel right to me. Books like Thomas Merton's *Emblems of a Season of Fury*, Clarice Lispector's *Agua Viva*, and now the Icelandic-Canadian Kristjana Gunnars' *Rose Garden*. Small is truly beautiful.

A Paul Klee painting, an Emily Dickinson poem, Jean Arp's concretions and his painted forest, a Howard Hodgkin bay, a Basho haiku, a Barbara Hepworth maquette, a Mark Strand poetry assemblage, these are all very small and all very beautiful.

Big books can be satisfying too. They are not cultivated gardens but overgrown yards. I love the natural sprawl of *Moby Dick*, a weed that doesn't know when to stop, roots that ramify everywhere. I love the girth of Camille Paglia's *Sexual Personae* and Harold Bloom's *Western Canon*. Big can be beautiful, as it often is in a large Henry Moore sculpture or in a massive Mark Rothko painting. That said, I seem to prefer small.

There's something very satisfying in squeezing the Cyclopean into small, human portions. Maybe the magic of making the big into the small goes back to my childhood when I floated pieces of bark on shallow streams. The bark seemed then like an ocean liner; the water, fathomless.

Gunnars has written a Book of Small, to steal Emily Carr's phrase and apply it to a physical object rather than a character. She is a poet of the small rather than a poet of the large. She excels in the short sentence.

Consider this: "I wanted to look at the Rhine River in the moonlight. I found my way to the riverbank by taxi. It was past midnight. The town of Bonn was closed for the night. Streets were empty. I went past the main building of the university and into the adjacent park. There was the water, flowing softly like a silken ribbon. Not as large a river as I always imagined it to be." Kristjana Gunnars is a noun-and-verb writer: few adjectives, few adverbs, but when placed, significant.

She keeps her eye on a single object until it bends into other objects. She gives her voice to those things which might easily be passed over and not be heard. In

– III: Small –

The Rose Garden, thought and feeling, self and Other, writer and reader, narrator and quoter link hands and voices. *"Let us for once refrain from hurried thinking,"* Heidegger intones. "Let us be still and allow the scent of roses to penetrate," the narrator mimics.

If Heidegger weren't in italics and the narrator in regular print, would you know where one voice trailed off and the other began?

Kristjana Gunnars' books are studies in the small. Studies of the small? Her mind turns to a word, a memory, a thought, an experience, a sensation. She shuns the grand, the theatrical, the ostentatious in concept just as she shuns the ornamental in style. If Vermeer's pictures could talk, they might sound like Gunnars' books: quiet, understated, restrained, memorable. She has written a small *Garden* filled, luminously, with small things.

Her *Rose Garden* is satisfying in the way that Northrop Frye once said a certain scene was satisfying. It was winter. Snow was on the cedar boughs. On one branch was a cardinal and on another was a blue jay. He felt that if his life suddenly ended all would be well. Why? Was it the balance, the wholeness, the colour co-ordination he felt vertiginous from? I don't know. He felt satisfied and sated. When I read Gunnars I feel sated too.

She invokes two of my roommate philosophers, Kierkegaard and Heidegger. Her book is full of quotations. She quotes effortlessly as if she were quoting herself, as if there were no difference between herself and the quoted one. The breath of someone else's thought intermingles with her own; her breath suffuses with ancestors and sisters.

I read the Heidegger and don't recognize it, go back to the source, and find she has quoted accurately what I have shamefully forgotten: "Is there anything more exciting and more dangerous for the poet than his relation to words?" I think of Emily Dickinson and Dennis Lee when I read these words.

Gunnars quotes two diarists, Anaïs Nin and Jean Cocteau; two writers, Marcel Proust and Antonin Artaud; two critics, Northrop Frye and Stanley Fish; two postmodernists, Linda Hutcheon and Fredric Jameson; and two feminists, Hélène Cixous and Julia Kristeva. Does Gunnars think in twos?

Sometimes the personalities in the book and their sayings clash; sometimes they harmonize. Artaud rages, for example, and Proust whispers. Weight and counterweight, balance is everywhere. Gunnars has a red bird and a blue bird on her green and white cedar bough.

Gunnars is a woman reading. I am a man reading. What you're reading now is me reading. My life in word, spirit and book. Sometimes I read other men reading: Donald Hall's *Life Work*, Dennis Lee's *Body Music*, Frank Lentricchia's reading of Thomas Merton in *The Edge of Night*. And women reading: Adrienne Rich's *What Is Found There*, which contains her wonderful journal jot-

— III: Small —

tings on Emily Dickinson, Hélène Cixous' *Readings* and *Reading With Clarice Lispector*. Women alone reading, men alone reading, a secret companionship with the word and each other.

Gunnars is a woman alone, reading in a garden, smelling roses, turning pages and dreaming, Proustily.

I'm usually alone when reading, but sometimes my wife reads with me. Sometimes my dog, Molson, is near. Sometimes I imagine Gunnars reading with me, a sensuous intelligence reading in full wakefulness.

When I have no one reading with me, or near me, I invent companions. At such times, the old monks of Europe spring to mind. "These men were readers," Kristjana Gunnars says. "Then they were writers of what they read."

Gunnars reads more than she writes. I read more than I write. I would distrust any writer who read less than he wrote. If I could only declare one nationality at the border, it would be reader.

I feel at home in a book about reading, about readings. Kristjana Gunnars is my soulsister, Iceland to my Ireland, ice for my fire. I feel at home in her small book. I like the wind blowing between her sound bites, between her photographic stills, between her poetic meditations. So very Japanese, mood and tone standing in for plot and character.

I feel I'm in a Kawabata novel with Heideggerian footnotes. I feel I'm keeping company with Basho and his haiku, Basho on one of his journeys to the north: the world as a grain of sand, the world as a rose garden in which she (the writer) and I (the reader) are Kings and Queens of infinite spaces.

Am I falling in love? Cheryl says I fall in love too easily, much too easily.

When I read Kristjana Gunnars, I know why I love reading and why the book matters to me and why I couldn't live without it. I somehow re-enact the primal scene of my first lovemaking. I fell early, and keep on falling. You fall in love with words and books early, or you don't fall in love at all. Sadly, I've come to that view, though latecomers and late lovers make a fool of me and my sadness.

With Gunnars, one word hides another word, one writer hides another writer, one book hides a hundred books, so her little book is made from a vast library. That feels very satisfying: how the big resides within the little, how the jolts and joys of the world are held in tense equipoise, how a cosmic reach distills itself into a rose's scent.

There's another hypnotic pull to Gunnars' book. She knits well. Sometimes with a single thread, sometimes with many. *The Prowler* works with a single thread, *The Rose Garden* with many. She knits the thread of narrative into the thread of description and reflection. The narrator, a female academic on leave, tells stories, shows pictures, displays thoughts, internalizes books. All in a single tone, a single mood.

– III: Small –

The way to enter the book is through tone and mood. You need to be on the narrator's wavelength before you play, and pray, with her thoughts.

Gunnars carefully orchestrates her music. Within the large symphonic music, she syncopates softer, quieter musics: a little Jan Garbarek within Arvo Pärt. She blends inner and outer weathers, she conflates the distance between external mountains and internal rivers, she weaves magically in and out of sounds and scenes. She whispers; her book, a book of hushes—wisps and whispers—the hush of a middle-aged woman in full poetic breath. She blows gently in your ear.

The Rose Garden is a blissful book. Gunnars writes blissfully, and you read her blissfully. But not perfectly so. There are a few irritants, a few discordant notes. Sometimes she tells you too much. Falsity creeps in. She asks if writing is not analogous "to working with fissionable material." Then she suggests writing is radioactive. Then she says you need gloves. A one-two-three punch. "Fissionable" makes the point; "radioactive" unnecessarily drives it home; and "gloves" buries it.

Sometimes Gunnars shouts. Thankfully, she shouts less than she whispers. If the shouts subsumed the whispers, the noise would be unbearable. When you read Proust, you hush because he hushes. Not to borrow his breath would dishonour the very one to whom you are paying homage.

Thankfully, Gunnars' book is not perfect. The perfect book is the end of reading. If you could get everything you needed from a single volume, and it travelled directly to your illness, in Clarissa Estella Estes' thought, and cured your illness, there would be no need to read another.

While not a perfect book, *The Rose Garden* houses perfectly rendered moments. As fragrances in a garden come and go, so the fragrance of Proust in Gunnars' *Garden* wafts in, lingers and wafts away. The narrator seizes upon the right sense.

Scent canopies, like a Christo covering flung over a building, but it does not do violence to what it accentuates. Sight may rape, touch may violate, smell may enrich what it infuses, but it does not fundamentally alter what is there.

Proust perfumes objects with language. The narrator perfumes herself with his words, her own words and the words of others. *The Rose Garden* is a book you inhale. All the scented words are windblown, all susceptible to sudden change just as fragrance in a garden is susceptible to wind-change. Everything, the narrator says, is "a poetry of breathing."

A perfect moment occurs again when the narrator quotes Heidegger on the meaning of the word "site." "The site gathers in and preserves all it has gathered, not like an encapsulating shell but rather by penetrating with its light all it has gathered, and only thus releasing it into its own nature." Then the narrator ingests Heidegger's words so personally that his "site" becomes her "garden." Like Heidegger's site, her garden "takes all things unto itself and keeps them...and emits them again in the fragrance of the rose."

The moment seems perfect to me because a dead thinker locks hands with a living poet, a site mutates to a garden, and what is first gathered up is later let go of.

Gunnars' way with prose strikes me as slightly different from anything else I've read. Nothing I know melds head and heart quite so magically, so musically. Nothing is quite so scholarly and so childlike in tone and texture. She owes something to Marguerite Duras and a dozen other sisters and grandmothers; she owes something, in my ear, to Hemingway and his garden, to the Hemingway of *The Garden of Eden* and "The Snows of Kilimanjaro." She sees into the underlying sadness of things.

Her music is strings. A deep, sad cello. No, I'm wrong. Her instrument is closer to her mouth, her lips, her breath. It is perhaps a wooden flute, trembling as she blows. Emotion and thought. Emotional thought. Thinking emotions. Gunnars collapses the boundary between prose and poetry, between thought and emotion, the thing and the mood it's wrapped in. She's simultaneously a master of mood and a maestro of things. She clasps the thinginess of things, stony presence within liquid evanescence.

I revel in her mixedness of things, in her elegiac tones, and in her books which resemble nothing so much as small pots into which she throws just about anything so long as the juices mingle. Her book about books, her book about reading, is a vessel for dreaming.

The Rose Garden takes you out of yourself, takes you away from whatever you happen to be stuck in. Your nostrils fill with foreign and familiar aromas. The book converts chronos into kairos, timeboundness into timelessness.

In her honouring of the small, Kristjana Gunnars soothes the senses and satisfies the mind.

IV
Revelation

Wings of Desire, a German film by Wim Wenders shamelessly imitated by Hollywood in *City of Angels*, enters your mind and doesn't leave it. Angels perch like giant birds on buildings, homesick, missing the everyday things of life, like a good cup of coffee, the kiss of a woman, the clasp of a child's hand. In the movie an old man worries about children not having stories to nourish and sustain them. He wanders through the bombed-out centre of Berlin looking for something. Is it a story? Is he looking for a revelation? Is that why readers read—to experience revelation?

I've just finished reading a letter to *The New York Times* this morning. The letter is headlined "Now Empty Bookshelves Mean Progress." The letter depresses me. People don't read because they're illiterate; they don't read because they're a-literate. They don't have the will to read. They don't care about reading deeply enough. They seek revelations elsewhere.

– Spirit Book Word –

How could empty bookshelves be a sign of progress? My bookshelves are full. Does that mean I'm regressing? Where would I be without Raymond Carver's stories and Emily Dickinson's poems? Have the new Germans not read Ezra Pound? "Man reading is man intensely alive. The book is a ball of light in one's hand."

I want everybody's shelves to be as full of books as they are of soup and salmon. Empty shelves, empty lives. How else can children fill their lives, if not with books? How can they find their way home without story-crumbs leading them to the door? If I found myself among the angelic orders, I would miss books more than coffee. I would yearn for the thunder of a good story and the lightning of a good poem. I picture the angels in Berlin reading.

Someone tells a story and you hear it. You hear it rumbling towards you from a distance, like a creaky apple cart on the horizon. You hear the faint rumble before you hear the thunderclap. Before you see the lightning. Sometimes it's hard to make out the central sound of the story. The narrator tells, characters within the narrative tell. Voices compete, overlap, intrude, interrupt, refract, deflect. A story in some ways resembles a play; it's a playground of voices.

You hear poems too. Poems make sounds in your ear.

When you're reading a good story or poem, you're in a storm. Dangerous things can happen. You're in a soulstorm, in the Brazilian storyteller Clarice Lispector's translated phrase. Literature, writ large or small, consists of soulstorms. To read is to stand in a storm.

Literary storms aren't quite like natural ones. In literature, the thunder rumbles and roars first, then the lightning flashes. You hear and then see, you hear and are seen.

You see a poem after you hear it. Or, more accurately, it sees you. It makes you see. You catch its bolt or you don't; it moves fast, it flashes once, and if you're not quick you won't catch it. You and your life will fail to be illuminated unless you see the lightning flash, unless you let the lightning strike you.

The story as thunder. The poem as lightning. Thunder and lightning, stories and poems. The elements are often mixed: good poems have a little thunder; good stories have a little lightning. Once in Zambia a young girl asked me what I believed in. I mumbled something. What I should have said was: "I believe in thunder and lightning. I believe in stories and poems. They are my sources of revelation."

Revelation, according to my *Concise Oxford Dictionary of English Etymology,* has to do with disclosing in a supernatural manner, divulging in discourse, making visible. In revelation, the veils come off.

I realize as I'm talking to you that I'm about to reveal something about myself. Something very personal. Something very private. Something I'd sooner not be so open about. I'm going to tell you how I read. I feel naked.

– Spirit Book Word –

A Flannery O'Connor story takes its time coming to you. You must be patient lest you too quickly determine where you are and with whom and get your company and your whereabouts wrong. Like a poem, her story is merciless; it doesn't give you a second chance. If you're not struck down, struck dumb, in the first reading, no amount of intellect is going to restore the potency of the first bolt, the bolt your body should have felt but didn't—because you were afraid, because you were hiding, because you didn't want to feel the lightning cleave you in half. Don't read unless you're accustomed to storms.

When I first read O'Connor's "Revelation," I heard some far-off rumbling and then some clear trumpet sounds and then a big boom. I read the story by misreading it; I read it by failing to understand it. The main character I thought was black, the man with her who limps I thought was her son. Why did I think the woman was black? Because she sounded black. To the untutored northern ear just about all southern speech sounds black. I also thought she was black because she wouldn't ask a child to give up her seat for her, and I couldn't imagine a genteel southern white woman not asking. Why did I think the man was her son? Because she talks to him like a mother to a child.

Was I set up to misread? Does O'Connor want me to set up false expectations she knows I won't be able to fulfill later? She wants me to mistrust my ground. Before making a fool of her character does she first have to make a fool of me? She wants me to read the story bare, without insulation. If I'm wrong about the opening details, I could be wrong about everything. She wants me to read the story blind: without confidence, without certainty, even without faith. She wants to shake my rafters and blow off my roof, and she does.

Isn't there a movie that keeps repeating the line "Are you talking to me? Are you talking to me?" O'Connor is talking to me. I hear her voice in my ear just like Mrs. Turpin feels the girl's eyes glom onto her and then her hands tighten around her neck. O'Connor is judging me, the way the fat, ugly, scowling girl with a strange light in her eye judges Mrs. Turpin. I feel it. A line from "A Good Man Is Hard to Find" comes to mind: "She would of been a good woman if it had been somebody there to shoot her every minute of her life." I take the line to be about Mrs. Turpin and me. With O'Connor, it's hard to separate her reading of characters from her reading of readers.

I read O'Connor sparingly. She takes too much out of me. I haven't read her one novel, *Wise Blood*, and probably won't for a long while. Not until I get the courage and stamina, and can overcome my fear.

In "Revelation" the judge is judged and found wanting. The reader as much as Mrs. Turpin. I think I know stuff, I think I understand stuff, and in my reading O'Connor says to me, "No, you don't! No, *you* don't. You're deceiving yourself. You're a fool. You don't know pigshit."

Do you remember the story? A woman walks into a doctor's waiting room with a man. She sizes up the talent in the room and isn't much impressed. She talks sweetly to everyone, even when her thoughts are sour. This one's pretentious and that one's white trash; this one is high society and that one's trying to be. She knows people by the shoes they wear. She gives a class analysis, in her mind mostly, worthy of Karl Marx. She's got it all figured out, every wrung on the southern social ladder. Only trouble is someone seems to be sizing her up. A girl with acne, very ugly Mrs. Turpin says, keeps staring at her, all through her social analysis and her metaphysical speculations.

Her name is Mary Grace. Mary, full of grace. Is this a joke? Is O'Connor telling a Catholic joke? Make the ugliest, most pimple-potted, anti-social girl imaginable and give her God's mother's name. Mary Grace holds up a mirror to Mrs. Ruby Turpin and makes her look. She holds up a mirror to me and makes me look. What Mrs. Turpin and I see isn't pretty. It's the side we'd rather not acknowledge, the shadow we'd sooner disown. But Mary full of Grace won't let us. Mrs. Turpin is a wart hog from hell and she has to come to know that, and I'm a wart hog from hell too, and I, as a reader, must come to know that.

Just when the avuncular Mrs. Turpin finishes telling the room how proud and pleased she is to be who she is, how grateful she is to feel grateful—"Oh thank you, Jesus, Jesus, thank you!"—the girl throws the book she's been reading at her, striking her in the left eye.

– IV: Revelation –

Then the girl slingshots herself across the room and clamps down on Mrs. Turpin's neck.

Mrs. Turpin regains consciousness and knows in her mind "that the girl did know her, knew her in some intense and personal way, beyond time and place and condition." She waits for an apology, as if for a "revelation." The girl, Mary Grace, locks her gaze onto Mrs. Turpin and says, "Go back to hell where you came from, you old wart hog." Ruby Turpin, "a respectable, hardworking, church-going woman" can't get the words out of her mind. She tells her black hired-hands what the girl said to her. Their solicitous manner fails to appease her. She goes and looks at the hogs. She reaches for a hose and sprays the hogs. She is trying to clean herself. She curses God. Why me? she screams. If you think I'm a hog, why didn't you make me one? If you think me trash, why didn't you make me trash? She stares at the pigs intensely until a vision strikes her.

She sees a bridge to heaven, from earth through fire to heaven. The first in line are the Negroes and the white trash and the last are the good citizens like herself. And you can see "by their shocked and altered faces that even their virtues [are] being burned away."

You and I are wart hogs from hell. The history of our century proves it, the history of our individual souls confirms it. And O'Connor won't let us deny it. We're guilty. We're all guilty. Only a deluded person would profess otherwise. There's a revelation in this story all right, only it's not the one Mrs. Turpin expects: not the one confirming her essential goodness and fair-mindedness, her jolly nature and her innocence. Rather, it's the one showing her ugly insides papered over by a veneer of respectability and charm. She would have been a good woman if someone had been there to strangle her from time to time.

Nothing is left standing in O'Connor's world of radical Christianity; there's nowhere to hide; no ground solid enough to walk on. All values are put into question when the first shall be last and the last shall be first.

Flannery O'Connor's story contains both thunder and lightning: a Babel of voices and a Damascus Road of Revelation. The work of Kristjana Gunnars, on the other hand, seems a much quieter affair: the thunder less noisy, the lightning illuminative, but not paralytic. Her poetry whispers.

Gunnars bears no resemblance to Mrs. Turpin, who now seems to have left her southern farm for the glitter of the art world and the games of the literati. Mrs. Turpin has changed forms and cloned herself into self-promoting, self-aggrandizing, pretentious fops, still cosmetically concealing their warts and denying their spiritual connection to pigs.

The untitled poems in *Carnival of Longing* do not, like a brass band, declare their own importance. Nor do they arrogantly assume clarity to be an artificial construct of the past to be gotten rid of for the new scaf-

– IV: Revelation –

folding of obscurantism. She doesn't play her own private language game at which the reader is invited merely to applaud. She has something to say to readers, and she wants them to understand:

> I do not want my words to grow
> and become important monsters
> I no longer recognize
>
> I want my stories to be small
> castaway bottles
> their contents drained
>
> no story can describe
> what it is to love uncertainly
> there are no words for those shadows
>
> how you stare at the sun
> how you take my hand in your sleep
> averting some private terror
> what it is to stand on the deck
> knowing forms are swimming below
> the surface of sleep

> that holding your hand will not keep you
>
> from sinking or drifting away
>
> and by some error of the imagination
>
> I have made words of a dream
>
> that is nothing but longing
>
> nothing but desire

The poem has mystery. Who is the I? Who is the you? Does it matter? Is this not a poem about language, about words, about what Heidegger calls the "House of Being"? Gunnars renames Heidegger's language house the "carnival of longing." Language is what we fall into at birth and out of at death; it's our Bethlehem and Golgotha, and between times we dream and long and desire. We're wordmade creatures. Our revelations come by way of language; we speak before, during and after the storm.

Kristjana Gunnars' words negate themselves, speak themselves and eclipse themselves, point to things and then erase them. Her poem clearly articulates the inadequacy of words, the impotence of words, while at the same time it recognizes words as the fundamental building blocks of the human. We word our ways. And if words are ultimately spectres, Ghost Dances and a chimera, they are still how we connect to the universe at large and how we express the deepest emotions of our longing and desire. Words are all we have to fend off the monsters and the shadows.

– IV: Revelation –

Watch the poet's moves. Seven stanzas, three lines in each. A mix of declarative, exclamatory and oracular statements. The pattern: detail, detail, a small climax. A build up, the way the air gets heavy before a storm, and then a small flash. All the details as breadcrumbs leading to the final door: the word as dream, longing and desire. The word cannot make or unmake or remake the real world; it can only make imaginary anti-worlds, counter-worlds, word-worlds.

Steal a theatrical technique from Peter Brook in his *Empty Space* and *The Shifting Point*, shedding the superfluous for the essential. Burn the poem to the ground and see what's left standing. Burn off the excess words, the modifying words and see the skeleton. X-ray the poem as the Australian aborigines x-ray their surroundings for art.

>   monsterwords
>
>   empty bottles
>
>   shadows
>
>   terrors
>
>   forms
>
>   drifting
>
>   wordlonging

Keep burning. Brook says *Waiting for Godot* consists of two tramps under a tree; *Mother Courage*, a clanging cart. What would he define as the central image of Gunnars' poem? A drained bottle? Is that what language is? Emptiness pitched into emptiness. A wish tossed overboard but emptied before it hits the water.

Now build. Embroider around the bones. Gunnars' poem connects to Dennis Lee's "Keep low" in "Blue Psalm," to Emily Dickinson and Clarice Lispector in their terror of saying a false word, and to Gaston Bachelard and his theory of poetry as a form of daydreaming, and so on. Every poem, at birth, wriggles into a family constellation of cousin-poems, sister-poems, grandparent-poems. And, if the new poem is fertile, it too gives birth to new family members, and so words make more words, stories make more stories and poems make other poems. Language, the one successful form of human ecology and waste management; words, constantly re-used, recycled, remade into thunder and lightning.

Beware the monstrous word, says Gunnars. The inflated word, says O'Connor. Hemingway refused to use the big words; the bigger the word the greater the lie, he thought. Thoreau said certain words were blasphemous, words like business and success. Let not the children hear them, he says in his journals. They have sin and death in them. D.H. Lawrence said beware "ready-made words and phrases"—of the sort Mrs. Turpin uses—for they suck "all the life-sap out of living things."

Gunnars keeps good company here with her poet-ancestors, with Dickinson and Hemingway, Thoreau and Lawrence. Stay within the small, she says. Get a few syllables right. Leave the saying and judging of the

IV: Revelation

world to the Mrs. Turpins. Say the small: less noise, less distortion, less falsehood. Words can't do much; they're merely how we desire and long and dream; they can't describe loving uncertainly, private terrors or forms "swimming below/the surface of sleep."

Connor tells all she knows. "Revelation" is a showstopper, a home run, a touchdown. The story calls for a radical realignment of the reader's sense of balance. You are not where you think you are, you are not with the one you think you are with, you are not who you think you are. Gunnars tells less than she knows. Her revelations are partial, piecemeal—unintended? Say a little bit, Gunnars says. Leave out more than you put in. The fox doesn't introduce himself. Neither does the poem. The poem happens. It quietly thunders from a distance, and then it almost invisibly flashes.

V
Quick

Quick. D.H. Lawrence's word. The word he was born to put flesh to.

Quick: akin to Clarice Lispector's now-instant. Quick: alive, lively, aliveness, liveliness, a lively aliveness. Lawrence uses the word in the same way the King James Bible uses it and Shakespeare uses it. Quick as in life-current, quick as in the opposite to dead. Lawrence has come to judge the quick and the dead.

Lawrence and the quick of things. All his tubercular days he follows the sun. He's guilty of many offences. Consider his sexism, even mild doses of misogyny, despite his having penned in *The Rainbow* one of the most beautiful lesbian scenes in world literature. But he never deserts the sun. He radiates, he glows, he burns. He has the sun as his centre. Where the sun is, life is. When it melts down, things quicken. When it clouds over, things freeze up. Lawrence sizes up the person by his potential for solar power:

> it is only immoral
>
> to be dead-alive,

Spirit Book Word

    sun-extinct

    and busy putting out the sun

    in other people.

He himself cursed more than he blessed sometimes. But you forgive the faults. He was cursed more than he was blessed, and in some Victorian circles the cursing still goes on.

He gave a lot: some of the best short stories in the language, some of the finest poems in the language. Lawrence, a much undervalued poet. Who has a wider-animating embrace of living things? He touches the quick and lets go. He's the poet of snakes and tortoises and elephants, of snapdragons, lupin and hollyhock. He can make a tree creak and a river croon.

Lawrence comes to judge the quick and the dead, and, tit for tat, the little weasel critics judge him and find him wanting. The English critic F.R. Leavis knew better: Lawrence has more life in a line than they have in their collective fopperies, more life in these lines

    become aware as leaves are aware

    and fine as flowers are fine

    and fierce as fire is fierce

    and subtle, silvery, tinkling and rippling

    as rain-water

    and still a man...

than in all their tomes and treatises.

V: Quick

Lawrence puts a stethoscope to the heart. He provides electric shock treatment to revive those on the edge. He conducts autopsies to determine the cause of death.

Quick is one of those words you know when it slaps you, when you have a choice to make. Once, I was channel-hopping: the sitcom *Ellen* on one channel, a monk on the other. I went with Ellen. She has more life in her lesbian face than the broad-souled monk had on his televized tongue.

Quick is a word you know when your life depends on it. Something beyond mind. Something like instinct, intuition, knowing in the bone, whole body knowing. If you're in fast water, the mind shuts down or you die. If it keeps judging, its analysis leads to paralytic panic. But if the mind yields to a deeper knowing, if it allows for the personal quick to gurgle up, then a kind of animal intelligence takes over. You go the way of the current's will.

Civilization for Lawrence: a flailing, destructive will to control. A discourtesy, an incivility to greater powers.

Ali had the quick in the first Joe Frazier fight. In the last round of the fight he was left-hooked onto "queer street." The place where fighters go when they're lost; when they're in an unliftable fog. Somehow he got up. Somehow he finished the round. His hands and feet and all his body parts knew, in their deepest knowing, how to survive for two more minutes. The Greeks called it cunning, the cunning of the full being, the whole person.

Forget about genres. Forget about forms. Follow Emily Dickinson. Ask yourself this when confronted with a piece of literature: Is this dead or alive? Is it quick or mind-bent, breath-dead?

Lawrence has it, the quick of life, in his work. A fox has it in its walk. All the senses wide open and awake. All the instincts working. Better alive work bad (as Lawrence sometimes is) than dead work good.

You take your Lawrence whole: all his excess; all his repetitions, his generalizations, his reductionism, his shrillness, his hysteria, his froth and foam; it's all part of his lifework. No sun without shadow.

See the invisible binding quick in *Sons and Lovers*. Paul in and out of love. He loves Miriam, and hates her on the same page, sometimes in the same speech. He finds her repulsively attractive and attractively repulsive. He loves and hates Clara too. He ebbs and flows, tide going out and tide coming in; he takes a good look at the menfolk too. Lawrence, a master of human ambivalence. He catches the quick of human emotion, "life wild at the source," life as untamable as a Clarice Lispector cockroach.

Quick: a religion and Lawrence its prophet.

Lawrence's essay "The Novel" is his manifesto of the quick. The god-flame in everything. Are you quick, sister? Are you quick, brother? Bruce Springsteen is

– V: Quick –

quick, so was Janis Joplin. Turn up the volume. That's what Toni Morrison said on *Oprah*. Turn up the volume. Give life a kick. Give your own life a kick.

Preface to *Women in Love*. Life in human form doesn't know what it's about, can't, too many internal wars and conflicts going on, so it moves forward and back, it builds and destroys. Character fluid not static. To write well is to be true to the wars, the tensions, the contradictions. To write well is to catch the movement of the ever-changing lines in the face. That's man alive and woman alive.

Quick and Lawrence's way with the word you see clearest in *Women in Love*:

"I couldn't bear this cold, eternal place without you," he said.

"I couldn't bear it, it would kill the quick of my life."

...and he wanted her to touch the quick of his being, he wanted that most of all.

...he could not touch the quick of her.

When did the word get narrowed into speed?

There is a connection: life's quick moves fast, and you have to be quick to touch it. I'm writing this fast, "mind leaping like dolphins" in Pound's phrase.

Lawrence in "Democracy:"

You can have life two ways. Either everything is

created from the mind, downwards; or else everything proceeds from the creative quick, outwards into exfoliation and blossom...the actual living quick itself is alone the creative reality.

I wrote a Lawrentian poem once: life at the end of fingertips.

That's where Lawrence says your life ends, at the end of your fingernail, your fingertips. He says that in "Why the Novel Matters." (The novel matters because it's the book of life, it has life within it, it's quick.)

Jack Kerouac has the quick in the first sentence of *Tristessa*, "I'm riding along with Tristessa in the cab, drunk..." Language creating life on a page. Kerouac and the present tense. He shoots a movie and shows it while shooting. He needs the present tense or the illusion of it.

Laurence Sterne has the quick all the way through *A Sentimental Journey* and *Tristram Shandy* where his moods race to keep pace with his words, because the words change him as he makes them. Very Shakespearean. Sterne moved and changed by his own words, his body a-twitch, a-stir to the bloodwords flowing through his story-veins. Too many stunts, though. Too much acrobatics. Is Sterne's quick confined to the daredevil language of his mind or is his quick a full body music?

Lawrence wants (and mostly achieves) the whole quick: the quick of life, of mind, of nature, of emotion, of language. Quick for quick. The quick in here for the

– V: Quick –

quick out there. His gripe with Joyce: Joyce turned sex into self-conscious language, *Ulysses* a dirty book. In Lawrence, language has a duty to honour the world: its physicality and sexuality. The word servant to the world, the novel in service of the quick.

Dennis Lee has the quick in *Riffs*. Clarice Lispector has it in her strange gaze and in her *Stream of Life* where she makes a story as she makes words. Emily Dickinson? Maybe in fragments. The quick for Dickinson slid too easily into instabilities. Hence, the formulaic, patterned poems. Protection against the unpredictable quick?

Thomas Merton has it in his journals: life on the fly. Gunnars has it in *Zero Hour* where her father is dying and she's telling you about it as it's happening, and she has it again in *The Rose Garden* in the fast movements between narrating and reflecting on what she narrates. The page, a performance. The book, a playhouse.

Wordquick/lifequick.

Orgasms in language. The novel, the place of multiple orgasms.

The danger in linguistic quickness is cleverness. Lawrence is never clever, or never just clever. He'd rather be wrong and slow than be a virtuoso.

Sometimes you want to fly. You want to fly, and you can if you get the words right—that's Kerouac's faith—you can fly if you get the words right. The right jazz and jive. You want to liftoff, blastoff, language dipping and diving like a drunken loon on a whitewater lake.

– Spirit Book Word –

Things go dead so quickly. Language too. The snap goes out. Words ossify. *Lady Chatterly's Lover* is Lawrence's big warm-hearted sex book. Listen to him rooster:

…all the great words…were cancelled for her generation. Love, joy, happiness, home, mother, father, husband, all these great dynamic words were half dead now…

…all the brilliant words seemed like dead leaves…

…sucking all the life-sap out of living things.

With dead words you can't honour the quivering quick of things. You make the fluid leaden and dry up the source-springs.

Lawrence is a maddening writer. Can you think of anyone more maddening? An oversized voice. Why must he always shout? He's excessive, goes on too long, gives too much—all those sermons in the novels and the plays, in the poems and the essays, in the stories and the paintings. Did he ever not preach?

Merton read him lifelong, and I keep going back, get irritated and go back, abandon him and go back and finally let him go, then creep back again like a drunk looking for a bottle.

V: Quick

Lee takes his measure of a poem from Lawrence and Merton does too. The poem: not a polished jewel but a jagged stone. A stone with a craggy face. The stone that rolls away the tomb.

Dear old Lorenzo. He must have been insufferable. No wonder Frieda made a shrine of him in order to keep his ghost from going on and on. Yet somehow he feels central, indispensable, irreplaceable.

Cheryl once took me to the shrine in Taos. She took a picture of me praying. I never told her what I prayed about. I closed my eyes and said, "Thanks, Lorenzo. Thanks."

He's so easily psychoanalyzed. A momma's boy wanting his mommy. If Freud hadn't found Sophocles he might have found Lawrence for his complexes. But you can apply Lawrence to Freud too. A man living in his mind, overconscious, instincts and boyjoy dried up, too much sex in the head, not enough in the body (Joyce and Sterne too?), a lack of balance.

Lawrence a hedgehog, a hedgehog for all his foxy moves. He knows one large thing: when something is alive and when it is dead; he knows the degrees of quickness, when you're half in the grave and when you're dancing on the tombstones.

Lorenzo as Zorba. He fancied himself an Etruscan or a Mexican, anything but English. Anything but the tight-lipped and the tight-assed. Did he become his word as a bulwark against what he might have been?

The word closest to you, the one you most need, is it the word you most fear? He wanted to be a dancer. He wanted to live the quick, not just write it.

He seems so un-English—he tries too hard, he's so very un-smooth—though he has very direct links to the King James, Mr. Shakespeare and Mr. Blake. Lawrence could have written the "proverbs of hell"; he comes straight out of *The Marriage of Heaven and Hell* where energy is eternal delight and without contraries there is no progression.

Mr. Blake and Mr. Lawrence, two working-class boyos prone to lightning prophecy and thunderclap revelation. Visionaries, Bible blackened, hymns in their ears.

Protestant rebels. Protestant heretics. Lawrence, the last of the romantic poets: the bite of Blake fused with the lyricism of Keats.

What Lawrence knows, he knows in fragments. No one sees whole or knows whole (not even Blake). We're parts seeing and knowing parts. Some of his best poems—crumbs. A slice, not a loaf. No writer gets the loaf. Lawrence's poems "neither star nor pearl but instantaneous like plasm."

He's obsessive over certain words and concepts.

He says dark and mysterious and blood too often and with too much seriousness; no wonder Spike Milligan can parody him in a booklet.

His lifeword quick, the word he gives vibration to.

V: Quick

Catch while catch can; he puts a pail under a waterfall, more water gets out than gets in, but he gets some in for a time until the new water tumbles out the old.

Lawrence subscribes to Blake's dicta: "Better a dead lion than a live dog." Is that Lawrence or Blake? I forget. "No bird flies too high if it flies with its own wings." I'm quoting from memory and probably inaccurately. "Expect poison from standing water." "Better murder an infant in its cradle than harbour unacted desires." "Arise and drink your bliss, for every thing that lives is holy." Lawrence is the only English poet who could have written Blake if Blake hadn't.

I'm in love with speed, the speeddriven-freefalling word. Because that's how I feel, and I look for places outside me that are like the places inside me.

Gunnars as poet: a photographer, a taker of stills. Click. Click.

The dew on the leaf. What the leaf feels like when it's touched and what happens to the dew and how the leaf feels afterwards. A series of shots. One picture then another. A slow camera, like the one in the Vietnamese film *The Scent of Green Papaya*. A book, a photo album. Can the quick be in the still?

The strength of Gunnars' poetry: the silence, not the speech. The space, not the fill. Words pointing away from themselves and towards their mothers.

Kerouac more motion picture director than still-life photographer. Stills sometimes within the moving picture. The language moves fast, too fast for the stills; they're overwhelmed; they can't last; you can't linger. Gunnars slows it down, slows it down. You can linger.

I want to talk with long spaces and extravagant pauses. I want more gaps than words, more silence than speech—more space, more space. Is that my monastic self talking or my quickening self?

Are these quick spacey words self-indulgent twaddle, megalomaniacal raves, or am I opening to the quick? Gamble, gentle lady, gamble, with all the dice you own.

Cheryl's the most alive person I've met. Lawrence would like her. I'd like Frieda. Cheryl's got life in all the pores, in every fibre. A man tried to put out her sun once, but he couldn't. You can't kill that girl's quick, nobody can. She has in the core of her being an inextinguishable sun. I feel alive around her.

Sterne and Kerouac scripting mindmovies. Time, no time, might die, gotta get it down before I do. Death the mother of beauty, and of motion. Words staving off death. If I'm still writing in the morning, I know I'm alive. Kerouac, unlike Sterne, can't cheer himself up. Words no antidote to his marrowbone melancholy. Poor Jack. Poor Jack.

Lee's riffs: shifts, tilts, spasms, gropes, plunges, muscles contracted and flexed, brow furrowed and unfurled. Lee wavering between a low cello and a high sax, Lee moving fast like a cat in the night: pounce, pounce.

– V: Quick –

Look at a lake and write Lawrence. The surface a silver dollar, then the darkest penny you've ever seen. Water purring like kittens, then throat gathering force, starting to dogbark and lionroar. Lawrence just about the best nature writer there is because he moves with the movements. The leaf blowing is him blowing.

The Quick and the Zen: everything now, whatever is happenin' is happenin' now—now, baby, ain't no other zone to zig in.

Sterne reading his pulse. Kerouac taking his temperature. Lawrence too reads his pulse and takes his temperature as he writes. I feel fine, I feel blue. Words alter sensibility... Jack falling, jackfalling, falling into despondency. Body talk. Words as body parts. Body all talking at once. The whole body talking, every part sentient, sensate, alive. Kerouac licks the world into life. Lawrence shakes it.

"And the sum and source of all quickness we will call god." That's Lawrence in "The Novel." As good a definition of divinity as you'll come by.

Sometimes Lawrence resurrects the dead. Sometimes he enlivens inanimate objects.

And there is a ridiculous little iron stove, which for some unknown reason is quick. And there is an iron wardrobe trunk, which for some still more mysterious reason is quick. And there are several books, whose mere corpus is dead, utterly dead and non-existent. And there is a sleeping cat, very quick. And a glass lamp, alas, is dead.

From "The Novel" again. Heidegger before Heidegger. Is his tongue partly in his cheek?

Lawrence walking among corpses, feeling for a pulse.

In the American edition of *New Poems* Lawrence stamps his signature:

> ...there is another kind of poetry: the poetry of that which is at hand: the immediate present. In the immediate present there is no perfection, no consummation, nothing finished. The strands are all flying, quivering, intermingling...There is no plasmic finality, nothing crystal, permanent... Give me nothing fixed, set, static... Give me the still, white seething, the incandescence and the coldness of the incarnate moment: the moment, the quick of all change and haste and opposition: the moment, the immediate present, the Now...the creative quick.

Every writer has his word: Kerouac go and Lawrence quick.

VI
Strange

Come in. There's a woman I want you to meet. A strange woman who writes strangely. Let me introduce her. You need to know her. She's clear light, clear vision. Welcome to her word-flesh. She's broader and deeper and braver and wilder and stranger than I am. She too is a writer of small books.

I stumbled into a bookstore once. On the shelf was *Soulstorm*. How could I say no? It might be the summing up of Emily Dickinson's life in poetry. When I first read her, just as when I first read Thomas Merton, I felt I was reading myself talking to myself. Someone had entered my mind and made art from my chaos.

For some writers, you need a guide. You need to see them through their very best readers' eyes. I see Clarice Lispector through the educating eyes of Hélène Cixous. In her latest novel, Kristjana Gunnars chooses to see Lispector with her own eyes, and then to see others with Lispector's eyes.

Lispector was born in Ukraine. Her family moved to Brazil. She wrote in Portuguese. She was Jewish. She wrote for a newspaper. She wrote novels and stories and children's stories, and chronicles—essay-stories or narrative-essays? How do you classify them?

Some writers immediately strike you as strange. When Simone Weil speaks, you know she's not Kant or Hegel. In a few lines, you know exactly why George Grant was so enthralled by her. When Clarice Lispector speaks, you hear a voice you may not have heard before. (I think I heard her once before in very personal words by Merton, but then perhaps I'm committing an injustice to Lispector, reading her through the film of memory and not through the necessary illusion of a fresh encounter.)

> I want to write to you as one who is learning…
> I know what I'm doing here… I'm improvising…
> I don't know what I'm writing about: I'm obscure even to myself… I write you in the very core of the instant…in this very perishable instant… Hear me, hear my silence. What I speak is never what I speak, but something else…

When you hear words like these in their sad and weary rhythms, you know why Hélène Cixous has devoted three books to reading her, and why she calls her Clarice.

Gunnars can't resist Clarice either. She, or her narrator, confesses to her seduction in *Night Train to Nykøbing*: "With my last bit of cash, I bought an essay by Clarice Lispector called *The Stream of Life* at my friend

– VI: Strange –

Jodey's bookstore." Is Gunnars' book an essay or a novel? I beg to differ with Gunnars: *The Stream of Life* is more novel than essay, though in either case, amphibious.

All through *Night Train to Nykøbing* Gunnars quotes from Lispector's *Stream of Life*. Lispector is her spirit-in-residence for *Night Train* in the same way Proust occupied that position in *The Rose Garden*. As Gunnars was reading Lispector, I was too, at the very same time. Strange.

When I find a writer with whom I'm congenial, I like to read everything by her. I read with my teeth. I tear into things with great enthusiasm. The Brazilian writer Clarice Lispector is not easily come by in my corner of the world, so I haven't been able to tear into everything by her. But I've read enough to know something of her strangeness.

I came upon Lispector first. Shortly after, I found Cixous. They belong together. The Lispector-Cixous connection is the closest bond I know of between writer and reader or between writer and writer. In Cixous, Lispector has found the one reader every writer dreams of: a Whitman found her Emerson. The one person who knows, and appreciates, all her moves and insights, who seems to internalize her intentions as well as her achievements.

Cixous writes *with* Lispector (the preposition "with" is her phrasing), not "about" her. She co-creates with her. She writes as if her tongue is in Lispector's throat. Two tongues in a single throat.

Lispector has, as you would expect, connections to many writers. No one writes alone. Every writer is indebted to her ancestors: to brothers and sisters, living and dead.

She has affinities with Kafka: a certain finicky exactness, a certain worrying and reworrying of the word. She also shares an interest in "lower" forms of life. Kafka has his beetle, his bug, his cockroach—critics still debate the nature of his insect—and Lispector has hers.

Sometimes she sounds like Thomas Merton.

She has connections to Katherine Mansfield: the off-beat humour, a certain quirkiness of perception. She has links to Virginia Woolf in her interior monologues, her stream of consciousness, her subjective impressionism. And she has a strangeness of perception and language you associate with other Latin American writers, including her countryman João Guimarães Rosa, whose "Third Bank of the River" I adore.

The most important word in Portuguese, according to Clarice Lispector, consists of a single letter, "*e*" (is). "It is." Hers is not entirely the God of Abraham or the God of Jesus, but, more precisely, the God of It and Is. She follows the Jewish tradition of not-naming divinity. "A name is an accretion," she says in her Passion story; "it inhibits contact with the thing." Her main character in *The Passion According to G.H.* has no name;

VI: Strange

she has initials. Lispector honours the strangeness of Being. The strangeness of beings in the perishable now.

She tires you out with her incessant interrogations, her radical realignments of vision. "Lispectorvision." Luckily, she writes thin books. Fat ones would be unendurable.

If you can imagine Heidegger being capable of writing a novel, you might imagine him writing *The Passion According to G.H.*, Lispector's most Heideggerian of works. Here she is more interested in the aura of the object than in the object itself, more interested in the effect of the object on the viewer than in either the object itself or the viewer herself. Here she manages to collapse the barriers between her body and the body of the Other and between her own physical body and her body of work to such an extent that she seems to give herself away. She gives away more of her body parts on the page than you can imagine somebody being brave enough to give.

I live for those moments when a strange voice raps on my ear, when a new style insinuates itself into my sensibility. When Lispector came a-knocking, I heard her. I love the sound of her Portuguese and the look of it: "*Fui ao encontro de mim.... Simplesmente eu sou eu. E você é você.... Olha para mim e me ama, Não: tu olhas para ti e te amas.*" (I went to an encounter with myself.... I am simply me. And you are you.... Look at me and love, No: you look at yourself and love yourself.)

Clarice Lispector has a genius for openings. From *The Stream of Life (Agua viva)*: "It's with such intense joy. It's such an hallelujah. 'Hallelujah,' I shout, an hallelujah that fuses with the darkest human howl..." *The Stream of Life* (I'd prefer *Lifewater* as the English translation) is her speediest novel, like a Jack Kerouac mind-movie. Written fast. Very fast. If there is an object in the novel, it is language itself. What the speaker speaks affects, moment to moment, her speech, alters her perception and personality. The speech act makes the speaker rather than the other way round.

From *The Hour of the Star*: "Everything in the world began with a yes."

From *The Passion According to G.H.*: "I keep looking, looking."

Strange openings.

Clarice concocts strange titles, or rather strange alternate titles. She says *The Hour of the Star* can also be called:

>   The Blame is Mine
>
>   Let Her Fend for Herself
>
>   ...
>
>   Singing the Blues
>
>   She Doesn't Know How to Protest
>
>   A Sense of Loss
>
>   ...

– VI: Strange –

Any one of the suggested titles—some whimsical, others rueful—is appropriate for a novel about a poor girl stumbling blindly through her life in the company of her poor, but oppressive, boyfriend. I rather like the Chekhovian "A Sense of Loss."

Clarice whispers strange asides to readers. Take this one from *The Passion According to G.H.*, for instance.

> This is a book just like any other book. But I would be happy if it were read only by people whose outlook is fully formed. People who know that an approach—to anything whatsoever—must be carried out gradually and laboriously, that it must traverse even the very opposite of what is being approached. They and they alone will, slowly, come to understand that this book exacts nothing of anyone. Over time, the character G.H. came to give me, for example, a very difficult pleasure; but it is called pleasure.

You can say the obverse of each statement (I read with Hélène Cixous here), and come as close to the novel as Lispector's affirmation comes. The book is like no other. Who has a fully formed outlook? How can an approach traverse the opposite of what it approaches? The book exacts everything from the reader: not just his mind, but his sense of being and Being. As for pleasure, yes, if pleasure is inseparable from pain. And why does Clarice sound like just another reader of G.H. rather than her creator?

Clarice records strange epigraphs. This from *G.H.*: "A complete life may be one ending in so full identification with the non-self that there is no self to die." The statement originates from the art critic Bernard Berenson. Lispector doesn't specify the source. I scour my library. I serendipitously, and very happily, come upon my first edition of *Sketch for a Self-Portrait*. On page 21, I find the quoted words. What is Clarice doing reading Berenson? She claimed not to have read much beyond her teens.

The narrator in *The Passion According to G.H.* does identify so closely with a cockroach—the lowest of the lows, a universal symbol of filth, a creature at once prelinguistic, prehistoric and prehuman—that when it dies the narrator "dies" too. Specifically, the narrator's will-to-humanize, which insists on separating higher lifeforms from lower ones, dies. Her self melds into the non-self of the cockroach. She surrenders herself to Life—not to her personal human life—but to the It which serves as the spawning ground of all living things.

Clarice deploys strange language. One of her translators, Ronald W. Sousa, talks about the untranslatability of her language, Portuguese but not Portuguese. A Portuguese she makes up as she goes. He speaks of her artful violations of language norms, her deliberate ambiguity and idiosyncrasy. He "invites the reader to imagine a Portuguese text that transmits a much greater sense of potential language chaos than does the translation." He even wonders aloud if what he has done can be called a "translation." But then he says in reference to *The Passion According to G.H.* "that undecidability is only fitting in regard to a work that may or may not be called a 'novel.'"

It's not easy naming what Clarice Lispector does. She herself in her journalism—she wrote a weekly column for *Jornal do Brasil*—wondered if what she wrote was a narrative? a dialogue? or a resume of her state of mind? Her columns were much admired, and she received letters about them and personal gifts for them. The gifts were for her openness and honesty and her risking nakedness for the reader's sake.

With respect to her novel about a woman designated by her initials and her relationship with a cockroach she ends up crushing and eating, Lispector begins each new chapter with the concluding sentence of the preceding chapter. Continuity and change. Sound and echo. She writes over 170 pages on a cockroach, maybe three times as long as Kafka's narrative.

She might have queried her narrative in the same way she queries her journalism: is it a philosophic treatise? an investigation into ontology? a personal crisis? a universal crisis? a psychological breakdown or a psychological breakthrough? a descent into madness or an ascent into insight? All of the above?

Lispector imagines strange stories. One story is called "The Smallest Woman In The World." Sounds like it might be from *The National Inquirer*, doesn't it? The story is about a 17-and-3/4-inch pregnant pygmy. The pygmy's happiest moment each morning is in the realization that she hasn't been eaten the night before. Clarice takes something unbelievable (extreme smallness) and adds something even more unbelievable to it (pregnancy) so that the story somehow seems more believable.

Soon you'll be able to say "strange as Lispector" as a proverb or an axiom.

Lispector's imaginative world consists of: horses, insects, cigarettes, God, hell, law, is, the now-instant, it, small, I, love, numbers, language, the impure, placenta or plasma, soulstorms, breath.

She loved animals and as a child was called "The Protector of Animals." Animals adapt themselves more easily to "the grace of existence," she says.

I want to say something about three words: is, it and the now-instant. The last item in my Heideggerian list is the easiest. Her now-instant is similar to D.H. Lawrence's quick. The now of life. Nowness. Clarice is interested in the immediacy of feeling and perception before language blunts it into a predictable pattern or an habitual repetition. Her narrators and her characters are often rendered speechless.

VI: Strange

The verb "to be" is key to much of Lispector's work, as it is in Heidegger's work. Things are. We are. "The grace of existence" is her lovely coinage. We find ourselves existing by grace. We find ourselves existing in the company of other beings who, by grace, are related to us.

As for "it," so much of life is "it" in Lispector. There is more it than I, more non-self than self, more non-person than person. Though, to complicate things a little, Hélène Cixous reminds me that cockroach in English, an it, is *barata* in Portuguese, a feminine noun. *The Passion According to G.H.*, then, on one level is a she talking to a she, a woman eating a woman. Even so, Lispector makes the Other non-personal and non-human on other levels. "Deep prayer," she writes in *The Stream of Life*, "is a meditation on the void. It's dry, electric contact with self, an impersonal self."

Is a book only comprehensible through the template of another book? Is it necessary to read *The Passion* with *The Stream* in hand? Revealingly, Lispector's narrator in *The Stream of Life* says, "I don't humanize animals because it's a crime...what I do is I animalize myself."

Lispector celebrates the it-factor of life, that which is alien and even repugnant to the human form of Being. She makes no effort, and sees no reason, to convert "it" into "thou," no need to inflate or deflate, idealize or denigrate. Things are, and they are different, and marvellous, by nature, even something as repulsive as a cockroach. "I need to feel the it of the animals again," Lispector says through her narrator in *The Stream of Life*.

Lispector is dangerous in her work, daring, even at times near madness. Once when I had too much to drink, I thought I had invaded her language, crawled inside it the way the narrator G.H. thinks she communes with the cockroach. I had entered her mind… leapt when it leapt…paused where it paused…no doubt a delusion but maybe a necessary one when reading a writer determined to make you see without protection.

Clarice's books are personal. They are talking books—an I speaks to a you. She assumes intimacy, as Kristjana Gunnars and Thomas Merton do in their work. The books also give the appearance of being unsure of themselves, not quite sure of their own nature. So often in Lispector's fiction the narrator is shaken by her own tale. Events, if only psychological, discombobulate the speaker. Something has happened—the sight of a cockroach, for example—and the narrator is trying to recover from it or reorient herself towards it.

If every writer has a word that propels her life, then Lispector's word is the strange, though her word could also be the mysterium tremendum or the quick. In her context they are the same. The shudder at being alive. The primal terror and awefulness of life. The inexplicability and incongruity of life.

Lawrence's quick is everywhere in evidence, especially in *The Stream of Life*. You can even argue that Dickinson's zero has some resonance in her work. Lispector returns you to rawness, to the moment when terror and beauty and horror and love are indistinguishable emotions. So often Lispector wants to start at the beginning, before the habit of linguistic repetition has impaired sight.

In "The Egg and the Chicken" the narrator wonders if it is possible to see an egg, or see anything at all.

> To see an egg never remains in the present. No sooner do I see an egg than I have seen an egg for the last three thousand years. The very instant an egg is seen, it is the memory of an egg—the only person to see the egg is someone who has already seen it.—Upon seeing the egg, it is already too late: an egg seen is an egg lost.

There seems no way out of this labyrinth of contradiction, and yet Lispector offers a tiny glint of hope. If you can see by looking, merely looking as an animal looks—not judging or categorizing or thinking or understanding—you have a chance of accepting the thing, or even, as in Clarice's cockroach story, loving it for its isness and aliveness. To look and see means looking within a state of flux, within the now-instant before fluid apprehensions harden into attitude and disposition.

G.H. *sees* the cockroach. Not at first, but over time, and the more she sees, the more radically her vision about life and her position in it is questioned and altered. She sees an ancient life form, one which we've come to see as ugly and dirty and threatening. There's nothing in a cockroach she can humanize; it's completely Other.

Yet the narrator learns slowly to see in the novel without thinking-seeing or categorizing-seeing or judging-seeing. She sees by unseeing, by unwording, by violating conventional patterns of syntax. She sees as a horse might, taking in the cockroach's being as if seen for the first time. She sees by suffering: by killing the cockroach, feeling guilty for its murder and eating its flesh.

Hélène Cixous doesn't think G.H. either kills or eats the cockroach. The text is ambiguous. I lean towards killing because G.H. does close the door, albeit accidentally, on the cockroach, she does see white plasma oozing from its body, she does bite into it. There's no doubt, though, that the narrator believes herself to have killed the cockroach. She has committed a crime for which she seeks punishment and expiation.

Is the cockroach Christ? Is the narrator? Do both partake of the one mystical Body?

The narrator is one form of Being; the cockroach is another. But each form is so violently different from the other that they seem illogically to occupy the same quadrant. How can she and it exist? What can they do with each other? The narrator at first cannot reconcile her being with the cockroach's, but she learns to. She learns to see without naming. In so doing, she begins to recognize that the life in her is also without name.

Here it's helpful to read Lispector through Thomas Merton in a letter dated 1/31/65. He's talking about Lao Tzu but he could as easily be talking about

– VI: Strange –

Lispector and her cockroach. "It is the void that is our personality, and not our individuality that seems to be concrete and defined and present... It is the Not-I that is most of all the I in each of us."

Lispector learns to appreciate the cockroach-life within her: the wild places, the ugly places, the dirty places, the places not susceptible to thought-analysis or convertible to humanization. "God is greater than goodness and its beauty," she says.

G.H. eats the impure. She crosses a boundary. She ingests the body of the primitive within her body of sophistication, the body of instinctive movement within her body of self-conscious manoeuvering, the body of uncontrollability within her controlling body. The last few pages of the novel dramatize her new perception of herself and the world:

To live is a gross, radiating indifference.

To be alive is unreachable by the most delicate of sensibilities. To be alive is inhuman...life in me does not bear my name.

...pain isn't something that happens to us but what we are...The human condition is Christ's passion.

In the novel the narrator, G.H., whose foothold on life is Modigliani-slim, de-creates and de-exists ("de-sists" is her way of putting it). She de-humanizes herself and Being and the beings around her in order to see. She falls apart so that the habitual organization of the self into stabilizing patterns of personhood can be jettisoned. She sees into the interdependence and interpenetration of all living matter. Her final words are these:

> …life is itself for me…
>
> I don't understand what I am saying.
>
> And, therefore, I adore.

I don't understand, therefore, I adore.

VII
Zero

Emily Dickinson only uses the word zero twice in her poems, and a few times in the letters, usually in the context of temperature rather than numbness of feeling. In a letter to Mr. Bowles, one of her minister friends, she pens a poem that sports with zero as the bottom of temperature and of feeling.

The zeros taught us phosphorous—

We learned to like the fire...

Zero is Dickinson's word-in-hiding, her word-in-waiting, her snake-in-the-grass word. It's her checkmate, her snakebite, her paroxysm. Although she's much more likely to use the words death and soul than soul-death or zero, zero is where she travels to. Her loaded gun poems go off at point zero: cock, click, blam!

She takes you to the other side of number, the dark side of number, the end of number. She takes you to the spot where number and civilization have not yet formed or to the spot where they, and other psychic defences, are powerless. She takes you to the wild and primitive place in the mind where rationality, stability and identity are under constant threat of annihilation.

In Dickinsonian shorthand, "Zero at the Bone" guncocks in poem after poem. The single poem in which the phrase occurs, number 986, is in the context of the snake. The snake, "a narrow Fellow in the Grass," in many mythologies has a life-freezing power to induce, in Dickinson's understatement, "a tighter breathing." It's a symbol of absolute terror.

I enter Dickinsonian logic: Zero is a snake. The letter Z is a frozen S, the S, an enlivened Z. The letter S has the shape of a slithering snake. The letter Z has the shape of a frozen snake. Therefore, zero is a snake. Zero is snakebite, snake-terror, snake-death. Zero is the place in the mind where everything comes to a stop.

Many of Dickinson's death-and-dread poems, her snake-and-zero poems, end in the first line: "I lived on Dread" (770), "I lost a World—the other day" (181), "I saw no Way—The Heavens were stitched" (378), "I am alive—I guess" (470), "I heard a Fly buzz—when I died" (465). These poems begin and end in the same place: horror. The mind has already frozen, and it has nothing left to do but circle back on itself and replay the terror.

T.H. Johnson, the editor of Dickinson's three volumes of poetry and her three volumes of letters, makes, to my mind, a just claim. Nineteenth-century America hosted three significant visitations (with apologies to Thoreau, Melville and Twain): Emerson's lecture in 1837 on "The American Scholar"; Whitman's handprinted 1855 edition of *Leaves of Grass*; and Emily Dickinson's letter to T.W. Higginson, April 15, 1862.

VII: Zero

In her letter she wanted to know from her future penpal if her poems (she had enclosed four) were alive or dead. It's a key question for any piece of writing, regardless of genre. Maybe the central question with which to confront any piece of literature is simply: Is it alive or dead?

Rev. T.W. Higginson had never seen anything like the poems, so he wasn't quite sure if they were alive or not. We know better now, thanks to readers like Adrienne Rich and Joyce Carol Oates, whose essays on Dickinson have deepened our understanding. The poems are live current, with a massive voltage to stun. They are the verbal re-creation of snakebite or gunblast.

The critics in many ways have still not caught up to Dickinson, though both Harold Bloom and Camille Paglia in their nineties grab-bags confer upon her the status of master. What does Bloom say? "Except for Kafka, I cannot think of any writer who has expressed desperation as powerfully and as constantly as Dickinson." Paglia calls her Madame de Sade, though I think she overplays the outward violence of her poems.

If anything, the pincushion is herself; the pins are her poems. She may open certain wounds by writing about them, but, more likely, she attempts to ward them off by anticipating their recurrence. Poetic voodoo.

At any rate, Kafka or de Sade, she has the stature of a modern Sappho. She has given birth to as many poets in the Americas as the long-breathed, randy-loping Whitman. Dickinson the laconic and Whitman the prolix: Whitman, a word-rope large enough to lasso a universe, and Dickinson a word-rope tight enough to strangle a gnat. Poets as different as Sylvia Plath and Robert Frost, and even our own Margaret Atwood, are equally inconceivable without her.

There is no bullshit in Dickinson, none, no dross, nothing faked or feigned in her elliptical short-breathed cryptic puzzles, her coy teases, her thinking "New Englandly," almost every snake utterance commencing or finishing at zero.

Many years ago she knocked on my door by way of Dennis Lee's *An Anthology of Verse*, often used in high school English programs. Poem 214, beginning with the first line "I taste a liquor never brewed," was among the first poems of hers I read. "Inebriate of air am I,/ And debauchee of dew" are lines still rattling in my head from my sixties exposure. Dickinson's poem of "drunkenness," paralleling Baudelaire's prose poem on the same theme, is less a call to indulgence than an invitation to live ecstatically.

The poem begins with her characteristic "I." In the Dickinson canon "I" accosts the reader like a summer's fly. Her "I," too real for a persona, is a very different "I" from Whitman's, her contemporary. While Whitman's "I" strides the cosmos cockily, Dickinson's periscopes woundedly, outside of time and place. He straddles the world; she remains inside the brain's "Haunted House," and knows herself to be a "Troubled Top."

– VII: Zero –

Whitman the astronomer of distant stars and Dickinson the cartographer of mind, with its fragility and wantonness, its fractures and fissures. Can you think of two more different titans?

Whitman rhapsodized; Dickinson anatomized. She anatomized the precariousness of her own mind. Her poems consist of tightened springs, stretched elastics, cocked guns, snakes in the grass. Her achievement, leaning back to Orpheus, is to have found a melody for bone, a song for zero.

She was writing one poem all her life, one poem with almost two thousand stanzas, the poem of her inner life, an autobiographical poem as vast in its way and as thorough as Wordsworth's *Prelude* and Whitman's *Leaves of Grass*. Her poetic autobiography is no paean to inner peace or recollected tranquility, to the balm of nature or talismanic dreams and shamanistic visions.

She, like Sylvia Plath, is the poet of terror. She is the poet not so much of the crack-up but the lead-up to the crack-up, and the nervous anticipation of terror's inevitable return. She dissects fear and panic; she scrapes away illusion and deceit; she enacts the drama of a mind in terror of meltdown. This sensitivity to the wayward mind makes her more "real" for me in our manic-depressive time than Whitman's braggadocio.

Singleness of purpose. Dickinson penned a single Shakespearean tragedy in her writing life: with one character, herself; with one prop, her brain; and with one theme, terror. The poet, terror-stricken and terrorized; the poem, traumatized. Dickinson writes the poetry of chills which puts on stage the recurrent crucifixion of self, the mood-mauled seesaw-self, in full awareness of its terror. In her mind dramas, pain is converted to poetry; private pain is transformed into public medicine. The poet retouches her wounds in their artistic forms so as to gain sovereignty over them, so as to brace for their recurrence. Dickinson as tremulousness and temerity. Her genius a combination of tremulous feeling with a temerity of expression. Destitution and defiance.

"When did the Dark happen?" she asks in a letter.

And if she were writing one poem or one mind-drama all her life—in drafts, fragments, riddles, epigrams, word experiments and dramatizations—she certainly wrote in one voice. In a traumatized voice, a hypnotic voice? In almost every Dickinson poem you wait for the lock to click, the knife to twist, the snake to bite. She writes unadorned, with "a terrible simplicity," as if words were live body parts—pulsing, throbbing, aching, writhing. The poem of her life, in its 1775 manifestations, has to do primarily with terror, intermittently interrupted by ecstatic moments and cloaked at times in wry humour, combative iconoclasm and corrosive irony.

"Good morning, Midnight!/...good night, Day!" is how she puts it.

She calibrates volatility and slippage, breakdown and impotence. She breadcrumbs the route to zero. At times she seems to be writing for her life. Did poetry

VII: Zero

save her life? The scholarly problem of precisely dating Dickinson's poems results from her monotone; one poem sounds much like another; early Dickinson sounds much the same as late Dickinson. The mind and its parasitical snakes are her themes throughout.

In her canon she features approximately 23 poems on the brain, 77 on the mind, 38 on the head, 114 on the heart and 126 on the soul. There are many other "mind" poems too that do not explicitly signal the topic.

Take these lines for example: "The Outer—from the Inner/Derives its Magnitude—/'Tis Duke, or Dwarf, according/As is the Central Mood—" (451). When Dickinson muses about the "outer" world, it's usually the "inner" world she intends. When she sports with volcanoes and earthquakes, lightning and storms, her external objects mask her internal minefield, and the slippery slopes outside are really the slippery skids inside.

The brain-and-mind poems in particular—"I felt a Funeral, in my brain" (280) and "I felt a Cleaving in my Mind" (935)—are among her strongest. Clearly, the working order of her sentient organs held an ongoing fascination for her. Her apparent world-mapping—raids into Greek mythology, the Bible or Shakespeare—disguises the true nature of her enterprise: mind-mapping.

Dickinson is strong medicine. When you've been snakebitten, you need strong medicine. I would describe her as the darkest read of my life. If you need vodka for Heidegger, you need a light wine with a little sweetness for Dickinson, a late harvest Riesling, say, to perk you up. She made, in Milton's phrase, "darkness visible," but it is not a darkness a teenager would wish to dwell in long. She takes you too far down and too far out, out past where I knew instinctively as a teenager it was safe to go.

I reread her now, after a pause of nearly thirty years, with the reading companionship of my poet-friend, Dr. Rick Guscott. Dr. Guscott uses her biblio-therapeutically with certain patients prone to particular mood disorders so that they may see that a great poet has been to where they are and has found words to ensnare the helplessness. Dr. Guscott combines poetry with pharmaceuticals, Dickinson with drugs. I think Dickinson would be pleased. She didn't put a tag on her affliction, but she knew she had one.

Read a poem like 556 as an example of Dickinson's mind-mapping, her word-thrift and poetic armour, and feel far enough away from its devastating zero to be safely detached.

> The Brain within its Groove
>
> Runs evenly—and true—
>
> But let a Splinter swerve—
>
> 'Twere easier for You—
>
> To put a Current back—
>
> When Floods have slit the Hills—
>
> And scooped a Turnpike for Themselves—

– VII: Zero –

And trodden out the Mills—

Who can pack more punch in a poem than Dickinson? You swallow the poem, gestate it, and grow into it. Her poetry is almost pre-cognitive. You read it with the nerves, on the bloodstream, by the pulse, in the dark.

Read the poem by its verbs first: "Runs," "swerve," "slit," "scooped," "trodden." Sounds ominous, doesn't it? Then read it by its nouns: "Groove," "Splinter," "Current," "Floods," "Turnpike," "Mills." Do you know where you are? Groove. Industrial? On a train track? Ball bearings, pistons, pulleys? The brain running smoothly, then a splinter swerves. Splinter as in wood, as in flesh?

Something small, that's all it takes, a small part of the brain swerves, slips off the groove and...and then, derailment and terror. It happens easily and it's hard to rectify.

Easier to put "a Current back." The current from a flood. Easier to put the current back after all the damage, after the hills have been slit and the turnpike scooped and the mills trodden. Easier to put the current back than the splintered and swerved brain back in the groove because what the current does to the countryside the splinter does to the brain. And the brain, like the countryside, can only be made right after all the damage has been done. Isn't that the sense of the poem?

You don't need to unravel the metaphors in Dickinson like snarled yarn or crack them open like hazel nuts. Even when you don't understand each line and every word, you understand the general dialectic and dynamism. You get the drift.

A terrible simplicity. The phrase belongs to Emerson, from his essay "The Poet." That's Dickinson in a nutshell: a terrible simplicity. She comes at you "finless," like a bullet. The way I put it in a poem once was: "The eye blinks/Short bursts/of breath/How like a gun/Dit. Dit."

Often the gun has already gone off when you read the first line of a Dickinson poem. A splinter has already swerved from the groove. The poem—as in 445, "'Twas just this time, last year, I died," recounts a past experience as if it is happening just as the reader reads the poem—is after the fact. The past tense is always present continuous in Dickinson. Terror only hobbles away temporarily; it slinks back later.

For a direct wallop of Dickinson's terrible simplicity and her "Zero at the Bone," listen to poem 870.

>   Finding is the first Act
>
>   The second, loss,
>
>   Third, Expedition for
>
>   The "Golden Fleece"
>
>   Fourth, no Discovery—
>
>   Fifth, no Crew—
>
>   Finally, no Golden Fleece—
>
>   Jason—sham—too.

– VII: Zero –

The poem combines the compression of Basho with the sweep of Shakespeare; its energy is centrifugally charged in contrast to her usually centripetally charged verse. The metaphor of Jason and the quest for the Golden Fleece takes Dickinson outside herself for a moment into an allegory of the mind. The verbal energy is thrown out and then recoils into itself; it builds then implodes. The poem enacts a five-act tragedy, with a climactic unravelling in the middle and a sleight of hand at the end which obliterates the play and the actor.

This poem, as in "I felt a Funeral, in my Brain" (280) and "After great pain, a formal feeling comes" (341), registers the mind's slippage into zero. The poet erects the mind's idols and illusions, then dismembers them one by one.

A colloquial paraphrase of the poem might go like this: you find something, you lose it, you set out for something else, you can't find it, you have no help, there's nothing there to find anyway and you're nothing too.

Characteristically, Dickinson weights her language on the side of nouns and, in poem 870, on a single verb; she shuns adjectives and adverbs, qualifiers of any kind. Hers is the poetry of kernel and core, without the protective pulp.

Poem 870 displays the scenelessness on which several critics have remarked. The mind confronts itself nakedly, without props. The reader does not know the time of day, the season, or the landscape around the speaker of the poem.

The voice drones on, namelessly. The reader is not even certain who is speaking. Is it Dickinson? Is it an imaginary speaker? Is it a disembodied mind? A mood? Is it Being in the centre of Nothingness, or the other way round? Is it pain made vocal in the centre of agony?

No, you don't want to hand out Dickinson poems indiscriminately to children any more than you'd hand out snakes. I'm not even sure I want to plaster her poems on the walls of the Toronto subway, along with Atwood and Borson, Bringhurst and Lee. If I were so inclined, I'd select carefully; she does have her exhilarating ones. However painful, though, I would want my son and daughter to read her, all of her, at some point.

Dickinson conveys vital information. She tells you where the bottom is, "Plank by Plank" (875), "Bone by Bone" (599); she gives you "Murder by degrees" (762), and the "Maelstrom, with a notch" (414).

Adrienne Rich, who reads Dickinson so well, regards her as the poet of "psychic extremity" who writes "the poetry of extreme states, the poetry of danger." The advantage of this poetry of danger is that we readers can "go further in our awareness, take risks we might not have dared; it says, at least: 'Someone has been here before.'" Someone else has been bitten down to point zero.

Dickinson tells you life is tenuous so drink it deep while you can:

– VII: Zero –

> The hallowing of Pain
>
> Like hallowing of Heaven
>
> Obtains at a corporeal cost—
>
> The Summit is not given

> All—is the price of All—.

She tells you to watch your step because the ground may not be firm under your feet; she tells you to beware excessive calm because "When Etna basks and purrs/Naples is more afraid/Than when she shows her Garnet Tooth…" These are messages all need to hear, the young no less than the old.

Yet, for all the bleakness in some Dickinson poems, there is a strange exhilaration, a peculiar jauntiness, even "a casual brutality." Consider poem 1127 as an example:

> Soft as the massacre of Suns
>
> By Evening's Sabres slain

There is no end punctuation in this haiku-knot as if to suggest a nightly and unending massacre. The subject remains unclear. The reader fills in the blank. What is as soft as the massacre of slain suns? Could it be the mind, the splintering and swerving mind? The lines seem throwaways, casual, a prelude to the longer music to come. But the music and the image are complete: a soft violence, a subtle unnerving.

The four main pictograms—"Soft"... "Suns"... "Sabres"... "slain"—alliteratively lull the reader into what turns out to be, upon reflection, a disturbing calm. Sound and sense jar.

Often the dramatized mind in Dickinson—her poems are frequently performative—falls, swerves, panics, erupts or cracks, but all within a sprightly rhythm. There is a zesty despair in Dickinson partly accountable by the structural rhythm and rhyme, partly accountable by "A Wounded Deer—leaps highest—" (165), and perhaps a third factor: Dickinson's poetry has the quality of someone who has come through, who has lived to tell her tale.

In sly knowingness she writes in poem 816:

> A Death blow is a Life blow to Some
>
> Who till they died, did not alive become—
>
> Who had they lived, had died but when
>
> They died, Vitality begun.

In Dickinson's body of work there is more than one crucifixion—has any poet in English died more often in her own poems?—but there are also quiet resurrections, resuscitations, resignations. Point zero may be ongoing, but it's neither final nor fatal. There is the will to go on despite the periodic and dreaded swerving from the groove. There is the courage to see zero clearly, and to articulate precisely its venomous consequences.

VIII
Being

When I attended McMaster University in the early 1970s students used to dash out of graduate classes in religious studies with Heidegger on their breath. With their incessant babble about Heidegger this and Heidegger that, they insisted that he was a Brobdingnagian among Lilliputians. They always used his surname, as if, like Plato, he had no first name. He wasn't the sort of guy you could easily pin Martin to anyway.

I knew nothing about him then. It turns out that he was a Nazi sympathizer, even for a time a Nazi member. He was thoroughly duped by Adolf Hitler, at one point proclaiming "The Führer himself and alone is the present and future German reality and its law." When asked by Karl Jaspers, "How can such an uneducated man govern Germany?" Heidegger replied, according to his biographer, Rüdiger Safranski, in *Martin Heidegger: Between Good and Evil*, "Education is quite irrelevant...just look at his wonderful hands."

Catholic-schooled, even at one time Jesuit-bound, Heidegger withdrew his dedication to his teacher

Edmund Husserl in *Being and Time* because it was politically disadvantageous for a German Christian to be associated with a German Jew. He avoided teaching Jewish doctoral students. He kept silent when his Jewish student and lover Hannah Arendt was forced to leave Germany. He said nothing when his friend Jaspers was dismissed from university teaching on the grounds that he had a Jewish wife.

"A coward, a liar, and the greatest philosopher of the twentieth century," the American thinker Richard Rorty has called him. Certainly cowardice and lying were qualities he put to work in an effort to position himself as Germany's national philosopher. In the 1930s, Heidegger seems to have been more preoccupied with Being than with individual beings. His metaphysics overrode his ethics. When brought before the denazification committee, he tried to justify his early support of Hitler by comparing it to Hegel's high regard for Napoleon. The committee, partly on Jaspers' insistence, was not convinced and stripped Heidegger of his teaching duties. He never apologized for his Nazi affiliation.

During my university years, George Grant, a professor of religious studies, became the campus centre for Heideggerian thought. Grant had the courage to make large statements when most academics were happier with minutiae. One of his large statements voiced the conviction that the Black Forest sage who drank wine with farmers in his ski chalet and whom he sometimes called "the old bastard" was "the thinker who [had] most deeply pondered our technological destiny."

– VIII: Being –

The next time I heard Heidegger's name was in 1977 in Dennis Lee's work of criticism, *Savage Fields*, in which Lee examines "world's assault on earth" through the work of Michael Ondaatje and Leonard Cohen. I also heard Heidegger's voice in Lee's own poem "The Gods." His opening stanza vibrates with Heideggerian diction mixed with Rilke's:

> Who, now, can speak of gods—
>
> their strokes and carnal voltage,
>
> old ripples of presence   a space ago
>
> archaic eddies of being?

The answer to the question is Heidegger can. Then in the early eighties my friend Mark Garber introduced me to "The Origin of the Work of Art," the same essay which Lee uses extensively in *Savage Fields*.

I liked what I read, or rather, I liked what I understood. Sensing both my befuddlement and my fascination, Mark passed along a copy of George Steiner's *Heidegger*, part of the Modern Masters Series, and still the most lucid introduction to Heidegger's thinking. Steiner has subsequently added to his introduction in order to take into account Heidegger's Nazism.

I was hooked and went on to read what I could buy from the bookstore or borrow from the library. At this point Heidegger was someone I read, but not someone whose thought had seeped into my pores or whose thought I could inject into my own creative work. Then, while at work on my poetic documentary of the Trappist monk Thomas Merton, published in 1988 as *The Thomas*

Merton Poems, I found myself lapsing into Heideggerian theory. Perhaps the best way to understand Heidegger was to do Heidegger, linguistically perform him and apply him to my own work.

In an unconscious echo of Heidegger and a poet he admired, Stefan George, I wrote, "There is no thing/ without the entwining word...There is no returning/ to the moment of/precopulation..." In defiance of current theories that to overcome human alienation one had to jettison language, I seemed intuitively to stand with Heidegger: that there is no Being in human form without language. While language, particularly when clad in calculative thought, can distance us from Being, language can also bring us closer, when poetically realized, to Being.

In Heidegger, language comes from poetry—in Emerson's phrase, language is "fossil poetry"—and thought comes out of language. In *On the Way to Language* Heidegger seems to suggest that language is something we move towards; it is not something we have reached. Language possesses; it is not possessed. Heidegger approaches language the way a mother draws near to her child and a farmer approaches the soil, cognizant of the need to cradle the fragile. Language must be "tended, cared for, husbanded in its own essential nature," he writes, as if it were the ground on whose fertility our lives depended.

One of Heidegger's principal criticisms of our technology-run lives is that we exalt the calculative and aggressive over the poetic and meditative. The rich heritage of language succumbs to symbolic logic and computer jargon, and the rich heritage of human diversity surrenders to efficiency, utility and uniformity. Man is not open to a variety of voices; he speaks and hears only one voice, the voice of activity, the voice of control, manipulation and domination.

Take, for example, Heidegger's justly famous meditation on the Rhine. One of the mother rivers of Europe, it was once a river to swim and fish in, a river about which poets wrote songs and poems, a river around which people fell in love, married and gave birth. It's now primarily a source of hydro-electric power. A multidimensional reality dwindles to one dimension. What once was open to a thicket of interpretations shrivels into one interpretation. The river now is what it is used for; no more, no less.

We define by utility. Rivers are converted to hydro-electric power, agriculture is transformed into "the mechanized food industry" and nature herself is pillaged as "a gigantic gasoline station." And "everywhere everything is ordered to stand by, to be immediately at hand, indeed to stand there just so that it may be on call for further ordering."

This idea of standing by to be ordered came home to me in great force when I saw Edward Gibney's stone-and-wood sculpture at a Canadian Christian Festival in the Hamilton Public Library a few years ago. Gibney, a

Saskatoon sculptor, called his sculpture "Nature Administered."

In looking at his split stone intersected by a highway of wood, I felt I was looking at the world in miniature; the worldwide administration of nature brought to life in a single sculpture; the re-enactment of the Faust myth in material form. I was looking at the human penchant for taming and mastering that which is Other, the conversion of all forms of Being into forms convenient for and conducive to the human form of being.

A hush descended upon me. I thought to myself: does this man know what he has done? He has summed up 40 volumes of Heidegger in a single image. For wasn't it Heidegger's life theme that human beings would not let the Being of the world, and the beings within the world, be? The wood in Gibney's sculpture not only intrudes upon the stone's space, it also circumscribes it. The planed and riveted wood domesticates the wild stone.

The organized wood rips apart the natural stone, drives through it, undergirds it and canopies it. Gibney runs a highway through a mountain. The stone is a bound being whose horizons have been curtailed by another being. Am I witnessing, I thought to myself, the crucifixion of stone? Even the stones are no longer free; they too are manhandled. Their being is subject to human control.

VIII: Being

Even to understand one word in Heidegger, the one word he gave his meditative life to, is no easy task. William Barrett's chapter on Heidegger in *Irrational Man* comes as close to clarity as any other elucidation of Heideggerian Being.

Heidegger's world starts where Nietzsche's leaves off. He begins with a universe in which God is absent, begins with "the night of the world," "a shrine without a temple." His theme, says Barrett, somewhat along the lines of Milton in *Paradise Lost*, is man's fall from Being and estrangement from Being.

Barrett argues through Heidegger that there are two senses of Being, "the thing-which-is" and "the to-be of what is;" in other words, there are beings (things) and Being from which beings derive. The closest sense of Heidegger's use of the word Being according to Barrett is the Eastern Tao, the way, the Source, emptiness, no-thing-ness. To strain syntax somewhat we might say that Being is the "isness" of what is, that which gives or permits or makes things possible, that which allows things to come forth and be known, the Silence from which speech comes, the Ground from which things grow or are revealed.

The fall from Being occurs when the Greek thinkers detach things, "as clear and distinct forms from their encompassing background, in order that they might reckon clearly with them…" Things can be measured and calculated, but the thing's essence, "the thing-in-itself, becomes more and more remote from man."

In Barrett's words "the subject becomes cut off from the object even as man's power to manipulate the object mounts..." and nothing is left to man "but his Will To Power over objects." Being, so transformed into beings (objects), can be brought under control. The point then becomes not to appreciate, or be astonished by Being, but to manipulate its manifestations. Against such manipulation, Heidegger forewarns, "Man is not the lord of beings. Man is the shepherd of Being."

Heidegger at different points in his writing says different things about the nature of the human fall, our alienation from Being. A champion of the Pre-Socratics, he is inclined to blame Plato for corrupting our understanding of, and response to, Being. According to Harold Alderman, in a valuable essay, "Heidegger's Critique of Science and Technology," Plato gives Being the characteristic of mathematical rationality, and thus assumes it can be precisely calculated. The result is "an aggressive spirit of thought that marks all of Western speculation."

In fairness to Plato we ought to say that if he reifies mathematics as a property of Being, Heidegger reifies language. He gives language a weight no poet would dare give it.

For example, in *An Introduction to Metaphysics* Heidegger claims that philosophy took a turn for the worse by translating the Greek word for Being, *physis*, into the Latin word *natura* which came to be associated with things, objects. The linguistic confusion "marks the first stage in the process by which we cut ourselves

VIII: Being

off and alienated ourselves from the original essence of Greek philosophy."

Heidegger maintains that *physis* originally encompassed heaven and earth, plants and animals, man and God, and meant "the power that emerges and the enduring realm under its sway." It is "the process of arising, of emerging from the hidden, whereby the hidden is first made to stand."

Here, as elsewhere, if Heidegger's style resists easy interpretation, there is some justification in that he deals with no less a subject than the mystery of existence. Another reason for obfuscation is perhaps that words in our time have become too easy to say. We sail across language as a yacht sails across water, smoothly, unthinkingly, without encumbrance. We speak without forethought, with an unearned confidence, deluding ourselves that we understand what we say. We neither pause nor question as we speak, and silence has no place in our speech.

Heidegger, on the other hand, tries valiantly to rid us of prepackaged language and prefabricated thought; he forces us to pause, to ponder, to question, to rethink thought, thoughts that have hardened into unassailable givens; he forces us to re-experience primal speech.

Nothing is said easily in Heidegger and nothing is understood easily. Through his explorations of a single word—Being—Heidegger makes the familiar strange, and guards against a quick understanding of the word's origin, history and destiny. He wants us to think our way back to that point in Emerson's "The Poet" in which every word is a poem, or to that point he describes in his *Early Greek Thinking*, where thinking is not a means to gain knowledge but "primordial poetry."

There doesn't seem to be another philosopher in the history of philosophy with the possible exception of Nietzsche, about whom Heidegger wrote four volumes, who can think poetically like this:

> When the early morning light quietly
> grows above the mountains
> The world's darkening never reaches
> to the light of Being.
> We are too late for the gods and too
> early for Being. Being's poem,
> just begun, is man.
>
> To head toward a star—this only.
> To think is to confine yourself to a
> single thought that one day stands
> still like a star in the world's sky.

– VIII: Being –

The poem serves as an example of what Hannah Arendt in her essay "Heidegger At 80" outlines as his way of thinking: "He did not think about something; he thought something." The poem also serves to underscore Heidegger's habit of dwelling on one word at a time, about which another student, Walter Biemel, remarks: "It sometimes happened that, in one semester, we read and tried to understand only two or three pages of a philosopher."

Primarily what Heidegger the poet and philosopher have in common is a certain poetic understanding of language. Heidegger concurs with Stefan George's poem "Words"—"Where word breaks off no thing may be"—because "it is in words and language that things first come into being and are…" And it is in poetry that language achieves its fullest bloom, for language in poetry is not language for political or scientific statement, but language as metaphor, as our primal way of connecting to the strangeness of Being.

Poetry enfevers language into full breath so that it can be "the House of Being." When language fails, or rather when we fail language, by transforming it into slogan or syllogism, it becomes a "used-up poem, from which there hardly resounds a call any longer."

This poetic way of seeing and responding to things, meditative thought, Heidegger places against the aggression of calculative thought. In his *Discourse on Thinking*, a very readable spoken lecture, he makes clear what he means by calculation. He traces the dominance of calculative thought over the meditative to the severance of science from its base philosophy, and the tendency of science in Western Europe since the seventeenth century to meld into technology.

> Modern science's way of representing pursues and entraps nature as a calculable coherence of forces...sets nature up to exhibit itself as a coherence of forces calculable in advance...orders its experiments precisely for the purpose of asking whether and how nature reports itself when set up in this way.

Ever the inquirer, Heidegger interrogates accepted wisdom. "But is the manifest character of what-is exhausted by what is demonstrable? Doesn't the insistence on what is demonstrable block the way to what-is?" He wonders aloud if "there is a thinking...more sober than the irresistible race of rationalization and the sweeping quality of cybernetics," which he predicted would replace philosophy itself.

And yet there is an intuition in Heidegger that the more nature is forced to reveal, the more it hides, the more it is attacked, the more it withdraws, or as he himself puts it in *Early Greek Thinking*, "As it reveals itself in beings, Being withdraws."

The world is darkening, says Heidegger, and the essentials of the darkening are: "the flight of the gods, the destruction of the earth, the standardization of man, the pre-eminence of the mediocre." Even time itself, which has the potential of *kairos*, the self-forgetfulness

VIII: Being

of a child at play or the epiphany of a man at prayer, has become *chronos*, the father devouring his children. "Time has ceased to be anything other than velocity, instantaneousness, and simultaneity, and time as history has vanished from the lives of all people."

In the midst of the darkening Heidegger calls for the return of the poet, and in particular the return of a single poet, Hölderlin. It is to the mad poet Hölderlin, a poet to whom the gods revealed more than he could assimilate, that Heidegger addresses his pleas and finds his hope. In the first stanza of "Patmos" Hölderlin writes:

> Near and
> > Hard to grasp is the god.
> > But where danger is,
> > The deliverer too grows strong.

And although Heidegger would agree with Dennis Lee in "The Gods" that
> > we live within
> > equations, models, paradigms
> > > which deaden the world, and now in our
> > > heads, though less in our inconsistent lives,
> > the tickle of cosmos is gone.

he would not despair.

Admittedly, he does come close to despair in an interview (1966) in *Der Spiegel* by saying "only a god can save us," but perhaps that has been his position from the beginning. In both Hölderlin and Heidegger "the tickle of cosmos is gone." The spell of cosmos, and man's relation to it, has been broken. The point now is to re-spell the cosmos through the most innocent and "the most dangerous of possessions"—language. Heidegger exhorts us to re-spell the cosmos, re-enter Eden, re-name the animals, and re-ensheathe creation in praise.

One of Heidegger's fears is that before the cosmos can be re-spelled, the technification of language will lead to the abandonment of natural language. He says in *On the Way to Language* that "metalinguistics is the metaphysics of the thoroughgoing technicalization of all languages into the sole operative instrument of interplanetary information. Metalanguage and sputnik, metalinguistics and rocketry are the same."

Although his confidence wavers about the human capacity to resist the onslaught of a technological juggernaut, and his thoughts are sometimes cloaked in ambiguous phrasing, Heidegger seems to come down finally on the side of mystery: Being finally is more powerful than what any one form of being can do to it.

Ever the etymologist, Heidegger, in a late work, *What is Called Thinking*, writes: "The Old English *thencan*, to think, and *thancian*, to thank, are closely related; the old English noun for thought is *thanc* or *thonc*—a thought, a grateful thought...." In the same lecture he goes on to say "In giving thanks, the heart gives thought to what it has and what it is... It thinks of itself as beholden... Original thinking is the thanks owed for being." Heidegger's quarrel with modernity has much to do with its self-worship and its lack of thanks.

Heidegger's work attempts to restore the original shudder at being alive that early man must have felt in the presence of energies and beings larger than himself. He attempts, after the Neitzschean funeral, to resurrect buried divinity, though divinity is not a word he uses very often. The beholden poet and thankful thinker remains, in George Steiner's phrasing, "the great master of astonishment" who strives for nothing less than the re-enchantment of the word, and hence the re-enchantment of the world.

IX
Tremendum

What do I need to tell you about Dennis Lee? You know him already as one of the central figures of Canadian letters. How do I make the familiar unfamiliar so that you can read Lee as a stranger to his work? You need to read him strange, whole, and in the large.

He came to our house for dinner and an interview once. Cheryl made Chicken Catalan. He said thank you with such conviction that I thought for a time that his word was simply thank you. In the evening he read us his poems.

The world comes to Dennis Lee through his ear; it enters by his body, in tremors and waves. He replays what he hears; his body drums back the vibrations. Sometimes he breaks his body in half: the bouncing boy and the wise old man. Sometimes the bouncing boy and the frowning man beat out different tunes.

At other times, the boy-joy weds with the man-thought so that a hymn sounds within a merry-go-round. A child hops into the brood of an adult's existential inquiry. One body. One poetry. An undivided tongue. Charlie Chaplin walks into an Ingmar Bergman film, Seuss bebops with Heidegger.

The poet is child and man. The best of Dennis Lee for me is the manchild poem: a man's mind within a child's body, musically tapping. Lee hears to see. His cheeks bulge with the "mouth-joy" (poet Donald Hall's phrase) of good-sounding "body music" (the title of his selected prose).

Of the criticism I've read around Lee's work, nothing strikes a deeper chord with me than George Grant's "Dennis Lee—Poetry and Philosophy" in *Tasks of Passion: Dennis Lee at Mid-Career*. The philosopher blesses his friend the poet by asking him to make more honey. More sweetness and light in the spidery dark. What a thing for a philosopher to say: Go and make more honey. Go and play.

I need to tell you how joy shines in Lee, how ecstasy flashes, and how play so often slips into prayer. I need to tell you about his lifeword—tremendum—the bridge between his man and child.

I read Dennis Lee for his playground of voices. I read him for gaiety and intensity. For his marrying of child and man. For his sweet-and-sour words. I read him for his forays into primary human need: the need for ecstasy and adoration. I read him for tremendum, that large foreign word, that big three-syllable sound.

– IX: Tremendum –

In his skips and meditations, Lee puts flesh to how Glenn Gould once defined art as "the lifelong construction of a state of wonder." Wonder (or the Spirit) is given room to breathe in typographical gaps and pauses. Lee is a poet of pause and space, of spirit-wind, as Dickinson is a poet of dashes and lightning bolts, of spirit-storms.

I've debated within myself what to call Lee's sun-and-moon word. "Hunger" comes to mind. It was to be the title of his selected poems, which he ended up calling *Nightwatch*. The word "gods" trips in, the title of one of his most famous poems and a word he uses in "The Death of Harold Ladoo." Even the unsaid word "God" stakes out ground; "Lord," too, for its hushed intimacy in *Civil Elegies*.

I opt for tremendum. It's a word used in specific poems and everywhere as a backdrop for what's missing in modernity. Tremendum: the tremendous, the dreadful, the "awful." The holy quiver. The tremble at the gate. What Lee in "The Gods" calls "dimension of otherness."

When you're in tremendum, you know it. You're awestruck. You're gaga. When I listen to Jan Garbarek's saxophone in *Officium*, I know I'm in tremendum. When I read *Riffs*, I know I'm there too. And the same goes for the Night Songs and the Simple Songs in *Nightwatch*. These are poems very close to music, words that spring from what Lee calls body music. The words originate

— Spirit Book Word —

in the body and rumble within the body; they also chime with larger musics outside the body.

The phrase "mysterium tremendum" enters common discourse from Rudolf Otto's *The Idea of the Holy*, written in 1917. Examples of the mysterium tremendum abound in Clarice Lispector's visionary work and in the rock-bottom darkness of Emily Dickinson. Lee turns to the word tremendum in "The Death of Harold Ladoo," along with another Otto variant "numinous," and in "The Gods." More everyday terms might be the vital spark or the sacred centre, or, to be more physical, the shiver in the spine.

Otto defines the "mysterium" as the "Wholly Other." Tremendum he shies away from defining but he draws boundaries for the word. He associates it with "awefulness," "overpoweringness," and "energy or urgency." You don't own tremendum; it owns you. You are seized or cornered or laid low. You are in a state of awe, you are overpowered, you feel great urgency.

Lee is in tremendum in these lines:

> Nothing can harness the things which are
>
> Winds of the spirit buffet and play,
>
> Usher me home to the everyday—
>
> Because, because in ecstasy
>
> I want it all today.

He hits the tremendum note more often in his children's work than elsewhere. In the philosophic meditations, the absence of tremendum is lamented. In

IX: Tremendum

the children's skips, tremendum is enacted. His book for the young-at-heart, *The Difficulty of Living on Other Planets*, brims with tremendum; and, for me, it stands as his most successful integration of his playful voice and his prayerful voice.

"Because In Ecstasy," a poem from *Other Planets*, touches all of Otto's bases. It has a sense of awe, a sense of being overpowered and a sense of urgency. It also points to a mind/body divide that courses through a good deal of Lee's poetry:

> But work and the brunt of the world combined
>
> To loosen my body from my mind.
>
> Flesh had a thousand things to know;
>
> Mind had matured, and told it No.
>
> Grimly the hunches were filed away,
>
> Dimly the body forgot to pray—

Dennis Lee is a song and dance man: the mind at prayer and the body at play. He's a two-handed writer: right-handed Teutonic raids on the nature of Being and the Real and left-handed Celtic jigs into the nature of childhood and the imagination. Hands apart and hands together. The hands come together in a poem like "The Thing," where Heidegger meets Robert Service, and in Riffs, where it's hard to know if the overbreath waxes philosophic and the underbreath blows whimsy and spoof, or the other way round.

Serious poems stray into the funny books, and the man clasps hands with the child. That happens in "The Coat" from *Nicholas Knock and Other People*. The poem bottles the compressed power of Yeats' "A Coat" and "He Wishes For The Clothes of Heaven." It hints darkly at the Yeatsian truth that "nothing can be sole or whole/ That has not been rent."

> I patched my coat with sunlight
>
> It lasted for a day.
>
> I patched my coat with moonlight,
>
> But the lining came away.
>
> I patched my coat with lightning
>
> And it flew off in the storm.
>
> I patched my coat with darkness:
>
> That coat has kept me warm.

For all the poem's chirpiness in tone—not unlike a Dickinsonian chirpiness—there is an understanding of the dark side of tremendum and the alchemy of human growth. We learn, as the psychologist James Hillman would say, by growing down. The poem also seems to enact an early wrestle with the negative way, a way of groping in the dark.

The marriage of child and adult occurs again in "Odysseus And Tumbleweed" from *Other Planets*, a dual enfleshment of "famous wanderers," one literary and the other natural. Lee plays a two-handed music in this poem. Into a gay banjo strumming, he whistles an oboe refrain, so the poem's music turns reflective:

IX: Tremendum

> Come away, and come away,
>
> And come away alone;
>
> Follow to the living source
>
> Before you turn to stone.

Lee sews little prayers into his whimsical work, prayer flags flapping on the clothesline of frolicking verse. He hands Nicholas Knock, that rebel for the imagination where wholeness resides, these prayerful lines to honour his silver honkabeest:

> Frisky, most silver, serene—
>
> bright step at the margins of air, you
>
> tiny colossus and
>
> winsome and
>
> master me, easy in sunlight, you
>
> gracious one come to me, live in
>
> my life.

Is the poet here invoking a honkabeest or a god?

Lee is a poet of tremendum. I know of no other who brings the spirit more fully into play. In a line or two he can sketch a character and make him memorable to the imagination. Herman the hoofer, Jenny the juvenile juggler, Suzie the balloon watcher, Chica who plays all day, and Lucy the pig—to say nothing of Peter Ping and Patrick Pong—all have real energy and presence unencumbered by leadening fact and straitjacketing reason.

Lee is a hunger poet too. Hunger and the tremendum are his two peas in a pod. Is tremendum not the hungering for the holy? One of his speakers in *Nightwatch* confesses,

> Looking back—what made me run? What pushed me
> year by year by year

through all those loves, careers, new drafts and last-ditch causes?
It was hunger.

In children's lullabies and adult goodbyes, Lee hungers for wholeness and tremendum. Like his fictional creation Nicholas Knock, he grieves the breaking up of Blake's imaginative body of the world—the mind/body, head/heart divide—and the split between the joyful body and the troubled mind.

Lee deftly brings the great divide into poetic consciousness, both by performing it—keeping his hands separate—and by overcoming it, with the joining of his hands. I rejoice in the wedding of man and child. I rejoice in the poems where spirit canters into the pluck of play, and play strums back in a spiritual depth-charge. The man strolls onto the playground and the child opens the door to the study.

Throughout Lee's work there's a hunger for wholeness, a hunger to re-integrate broken off parts of the self into unity. In *Riffs*, he rings out a whole book about hunger from the sexual to the spiritual, and in "Heart Residence" the speaker confesses:

> I hear we have no home: No
> home but hunger.

– IX: Tremendum –

No home but hunger. Here Lee taps into a word with mythic amplitude and a deep Saxon root. Eros is too Greek and desire too French. And while his speakers may not know what they are hungering for, they know that within hunger, historically and personally, the human being is situated. Hungering is home. Fundamental human ache. The pang and grope of existence.

Lee's speakers hunger for something to adore, something to be in awe of, something to be in a state of tremendum over. The poem that makes this particular hunger clearest to me is "The Gods." You can number Lee among the god-poets, among those who feel that when you clamp the highest thought of the human imagination into a cliché, a father complex or an hypothesis, something drains from the vital core.

When you take away the sky, the earth wilts. When you take away the sky in all its metaphoric pregnancy, the human being droops into smallness and self-absorption. As Lee puts it in "The Gods," we begin to dwell within

> equations, models, paradigms
>   which deaden the world...
> the tickle of cosmos is gone.

Lee in "The Gods" likens the god-force to a bear. It's "furred," "hot-breathing," and "erect"; it stinks and roars and "rears foursquare"; it's an "old/force & destroyer..." The poem makes me pull my breath in. I know I'm in a force field charged with current, a savage field. The bear-god can rip you apart.

There are three parts to the poem: we can't experience what-is as sacred anymore; we might be able to if we resurrect the language for it; if we can't, it's "better to speak in silence than squeak in the gab of the age." Lines written for "Ladoo" fit perfectly in "The Gods" as well:

> For a civilization cannot sustain
>
> lobotomy, meaning the loss of awe,
>
> the numbing of tremendum...

Lee's work worships and adores, mourns and elegizes, without an object as either the source or the destination of the adoration or mourning. His work tensely swings between hope and despair:

> ...if I
>
> deny the slaughterhouse world—
>
> or if I deny the luminous presence—
>
> something goes numb at the core.

If the tension slackens, the feeling of tremendum, and the sense of the holy, loosen.

Lee's way of maintaining tremendum in his work, in defiance of rationality and contemporary history, is partly through the negative way. In *The New Quarterly* interview conducted in our home, and published in the summer of 1994, he says it this way:

– IX: Tremendum –

...religious reflections have to drop away just as completely as everything else; and where you wait in 'naked intent.' In un-knowing awe and desire...That approach felt like home. It felt like the one way open—in the West, I mean—in the age of unbelief.

In the interview, Lee specifically invoked the fourteenth-century author of *The Cloud of Unknowing*, the anonymous monk who advocated praying with one-syllable words. For while Lee cannot bring himself to belief, neither can he quell the stirring within to adore.

Intellectually, what he limps towards is a philosophy that authenticates the reality of hunger and the experience of tremendum, all the while knowing that rationality and technologically sculpted language allow little space for either. In the words of *The Cloud of Unknowing*, which Lee quoted from memory in the interview, "It is not your will or desire that moves you, but something you are completely ignorant of, stirring you to will and desire you know not what."

An aural poet, a ventriloquist, Lee works by sound, in sound. Tremendum enters by sound, and makes its presence felt by rhythm and cadence. The poem "Cadence," for example, approaches the unsayable by sound rather than concept.

> swivel and carom and thud...
>
> ...a leghold rumble of is.

Not so much image-haunted as sound-splattered, Lee's poems speed towards you at great velocity, in quick breath.

Some of the poems from his auditory imagination seem more zestful, others more plaintive, but all rattle in distinct voice rhythms. Lee keeps his sonar equipment in good working order, and as a reader, your ear attunes to the sonic booms and the subsonic sighs.

The sound of hunger pelts down like horses' hooves, shambles like a wounded bear or whimpers like a snared rabbit. In the hunger poems you don't say, "So this is what hunger looks like." You say, "So this is what hunger sounds like." Hunger whimpers, snorts, wheezes, gasps, howls and cackles.

Lee feels a hunger for something he cannot name, for something that in the present condition of language may be unnameable. His speaker in "Blue Psalm" lucidly hushes:

> For there is a calling, nameable by silence; and a track, a path of no-
> going.

Sometimes in particular poems you have the sense of a seeker overwhelmed by the hollow sound of empty vessels. But in a wide scoop of Lee's poems, you hear a chorus of celebration and acceptance within a song of lament. The result is balance: day and night, joy and sorrow—the negative way and the positive way harmoniously, even humorously, intersecting and crisscrossing. You have a meld of what Clarice Lispector

IX: Tremendum

calls "the hallelujah" and "the human howl," and what Lee himself in an unpublished poem calls "juniper and bone."

> Old momma teach me moonlight
> > Old momma teach me skin
>
> Old momma teach me timing
> > When the ocean crashes in
>
> And momma teach me heartland
> > And teach me highway fear
>
> Old momma teach me hunger
> > At the turning of the year
>
> Old momma teach me music
> > Made of juniper and bone
>
> Old momma teach me homing
> > To the certainty of stone.

Tremendum provides the bridge between two poles: the happy-awe of the child's dance blended with the sad-awe of the adult's knowingness. In poems such as "Juniper and Bone" and Night Songs 7, 14 and 16 in *Nightwatch*, day and night dart and mottle.

Sometimes Lee divides his poetry-making self into the child at play and the adult at mourning, left-hand play and right-hand seriousness. But often the hands clasp in mixed music, too. *Riffs*, with its adult themes and childlike linguistic play, *The Difficulty of Living on Other Planets* with its sound of one hand clapping, *Nicholas Knock* with its portraiture, and Simple Songs and Night Songs from *Nightwatch*, stand among his strongest manchild poems. The adult welcomes the child, as buttermilk welcomes a little honey. Sceptics need trust and mischief-makers need rootedness—like the Kitsilano Kid skipping to the door with Hölderlin in hand.

As an adult, Lee cannot fully embrace faith and belief, much as he tries and would wish. As a child, he transcends the mind's categories and freely abandons himself to mystery, while dancing rambunctiously. Listen again to the beginning and end of "A Song for Ookpik" from *Nicholas Knock and Other People*:

> Ookpik,
>
> Ookpik
>
> Dance with
>
> Us.
>
> Till our
>
> Lives
>
> Go
>
> Luminous…
>
> Ookpik,
>
> Ookpik

– IX: Tremendum –

> By your
>
> Grace,
>
> Help us
>
> Live in
>
> Our own
>
> Space.

What are these stanzas but an invocation to a god, a prayer for presence, the quiver of tremendum?

In unpublished poems, which I've been privileged to see, Lee more and more fuses his songs of innocence with his songs of experience. Joy and sadness waddle in the same poem, and sing the same unbroken breath. Lee is a master of polyphony. He has the technical skill to pull off a mixed marriage. It's not easy. Not even Blake was able to interbreed his tiger and lamb poems; they remained two separate musics.

Dennis Lee's fullest body music nests in the poems of his manchild. His strength as a poet lies in his blending of *Song of Solomon* with *Psalms* and *Ecclesiastes*, in poems of serious play and playful thought, in poems of hallelujah and howl. The words may veer off in poignancy and sadness, but the body's rhythms re-integrate them into the dance.

The core voice in Lee for me is not existential angst, but joy. It's joy where his rhythm and cadence come from, his bodily appreciation of being alive: of being here and not there, of being flesh and not mechanics, of being able to smell and taste the world. Poems like "The Coat" achieve this kind of manchild balance and harmony: a deep, sad say about the world within an infectious and life-affirming sway.

Can scholar and gamester, thinker and prankster, occupy a single body? Yes. In Lee the sound juggler, the manchild in tremendum.

As a body musician, Lee honours the world's sad-joy, the joyous tear of things. He carries the weary weight of the world, and lets it go like a birthday balloon. He howls and hallelujahs in the same breath. His child is father to his man.

Sometimes Lee's body seems to know things that his mind hasn't got round to fully knowing yet. Sometimes his left-hand has resolved tensions and obstacles his right-hand still recoils from. Wonder and hunger, the trusting child and the worried adult, do not always join hands comfortably in tremendum. Nor do they need to. A child would spoil "Ladoo," and a man would spoil "Alligator Pie." Each hand can have its own clap, its separate music. But when the hands oink and yodel together, they orchestrate Lee's most integrated body music.

The manchild poems—I'm thinking of poems like "The Butterfly," "The Secret Place," and "Silverly," along with the dozen or so I've already mentioned, where the body's dance mollifies the mind's self-consuming fire—show how magnificently the six- and sixty-year-old within Lee sing in unison:

IX: Tremendum

    here for a

    jiffy

    and then

    goodbye—

    butterfly,

    butterfly,

    flutter

    on by.

These lines are in tremendum: "slaughterhouse world" and "luminous presence" in full body music.

X
Obedience

George Grant begins his notes on obedience with two words: "suffers, yields."

Suffer for another. Yield to another.

Obey in its etymological root, *obeir*, means to listen. Listen to what? For what?

Grant, an Anglican, is a good listener. "George receives the question whole… he is penetrated by the question… body and being…" notes journalist Scott Symons in *Dear Reader* on his visit to Grant's Dundas home, with Dennis Lee and Charles Taylor.

Grant, obedient to a call. Swallowed by a succession of whales: Leo Strauss, Martin Heidegger, Simone Weil. He thinks within thinkers larger than himself, the way Frye thinks within Blake, as if within his belly, the way Cixous thinks within Lispector. Grant comes to think within Weil, within the Gospels.

Grant, beholden to the Gospels. What does Clarice Lispector say? "The Passion of Christ is the human condition." Grant believed that the Stations of the Cross were the stages through which human beings unavoidably passed.

Obedience is one of the key words in the New Testament. Paul speaks of "obedience to faith," "obedience unto righteousness," "every thought to obedience of Christ," "Christ became obedient to death." The Old Testament says "be obedient to his voice."

To what voices am I obedient? Raymond Carver and Thomas Merton were obedient to the call of writing.

Obedient as a dog. Obedience is one of the dead words, one of the funereal words buried deep in Nietzsche's coffin, along with grace and the good, along with all the word-signs of transcendence.

No authority, therefore, no obedience.

Obedience: abbots and monks, coaches and athletes, masters and disciples...dogs... more? Poets. Emily Dickinson was, and Dennis Lee is, obedient to the call of poetry.

Is obedience desirable? At what cost to freedom? Obedience to an idea is often dangerous. Witness Christian, Islamic and Jewish fundamentalism: the willingness to live and die for an idea (Kierkegaard) and to kill for an idea (Marx).

And yet: the metaphysical need for obedience exists beyond the whines of the self. Perhaps there is an unresolvable tension between freedom and obedience. Paul says you find your freedom in service: obedience

— X: Obedience —

a necessary check on freedom, a necessary restraint on the ravenous ego. Faust, Don Juan, Satan, Lady Macbeth, Edmund, Iago, Richard III, Raskolnikov have no obedience. They have no obedience; therefore, they have no limits.

Is our time a time of no obedience, a space with no horizon? Swiftian Free-Thinkers, the kind Swift parodies in his *Tale of a Tub*, seem let loose upon the world. Isn't the liberal dream the dream of the individual's unfettered thought, thinking without boundaries and traditions? You can think anything, say anything, do anything. Grant comes down on the side of the ancients in the battle of the books: memory over novelty, obedience over license. No thought is free. There are no "free" thinkers.

Christ's voice is full of calls to obedience: give what you have to the poor, turn the other cheek, go the second mile, take up your bed and walk, go down to the Jordan and put mud in your eye—you'll see better. Absurdist Zen calls. Profound radical calls for re-visioning, re-valuing, self-overcoming. Calls to risk. Calls to give up your life for another.

To what am I obedient? Obedient to a few words I'm only just beginning to know how to spell and feel with and dream by?

With notes you enter the inner sanctum where the soul is being forged: the first flailings of the soul, the birth-groans of a new lifeform. Embryonic thought, uterine thought, Grant is at his best womb-wet. The writer as Adam, the word as Eden.

Me, I'm writing notes on notes, sliver for sliver, crumb for crumb.

Grant's words orbit like planets. No word is in isolation, no word is sisterless. Each word is held in place by the gravity of another. Obedience after all belongs to the cosmos of belief and the stars of faith; it spins by grace; it shines by love. For Grant, obedience is the sunword; its radiance lights up a sky-language, yet it's dark, the dark sun, too—it demands, it compels.

There is something beautiful in broken sentences, something beautiful about unfinished symphonies, unfinished sculptures, unfinished books. Remember Michelangelo's slave sculptures, the slaves breaking out of the stone, half-finished, half-free—the rough and the smooth, the given and the made. Magnificent sculpture, the stronger for its unfinishedness. You see the purity of line, the purity of intention, the respect for the given. The same quality exists in many of Noguchi's sculptures, stones partly shaped and polished and partly left alone, allowed to be.

Someday I would like to visit Isamu Noguchi in Long Island, visit his stones.

In 1990, two years after Grant's death, the Toronto magazine *The Idler* published some of Grant's thoughts centred around the theme of obedience. The notes were found in a box marked "Grant's Notes on Techné—Book." Grant's wife, Sheila Grant, helped the editor of the magazine, Gerald Owen, organize the notes. They

X: Obedience

were set down as if they were a draft towards a poem. There is something very human in notes; they give you the feeling that life goes on, that it never finishes, that it can't be polished, that moving towards things is about as good as you can get. Staying open. You stop but things go on. Someone else can pick up your thoughts and run with them; they can spit-shine them into paragraphs and essays and blocks of systematic thought.

Me, I like fragments, crumbs, embryos. I like the inchoate, the first visitations of the Rilkean angel. I like laments and elegies. Much of George Grant's work is a lament, much of his friend Dennis Lee's work is an elegy.

Grant didn't write easily. No anodynes for the masses for him. He was often badgered by Lee into it. Grant was a talker. He liked to rail against the cretins. Writing takes discipline, concentration, a beavering down not always congenial to a gabber. The best of Grant consists of words composed on the tongue. Much of his work consists of public lectures on the CBC or at universities. Grant was a public thinker, an engaged thinker, a man of patrician upbringing who wanted to speak to workers and students.

Once I passed by his office at McMaster University, and I could hear him from a long way off. He spoke loudly as if he were on the stage at Stratford, bellowing like Lear. I overheard him talk about Wyndham Lewis' visit to Toronto and about bridge. Whatever he pontificated on, he projected with excessive gusto. More Falstaff than Lear, he talked mightily, with authority and theatricality. He adhered to Martin Luther's line "live in the large! dare greatly, and if you must sin, sin nobly."

On another occasion I heard him speak about Vietnam, on campus, in 1969, I believe. He looked "old and dirty and fat." A Bogartian cigarette dangled from his mouth as he spoke. The lecture theatre was packed; students were at his feet, betting on the falling of ash. I knew vaguely then that I was in the presence of power. He spoke without notes, in half-sentences, as I recall, unfinished sentences, or one sentence interrupted (invaded) by another sentence. Nothing seemed to get fully said. It didn't need to. You got the message. He spoke with urgency, to the powerless, as if we had great power; he spoke to us as if we were his equals or co-conspirators.

When you read Grant, you have this sense of urgency, too. Read this. Understand it. Change your life. Do something.

He didn't write much: a half-dozen books, two with Dennis Lee's publisher, House of Anansi. All the books were thin, all around 100 pages, and the most dense of all, the one on Nietzsche, 52 pages. The Nietzsche book was called *Time as History* for the CBC's Massey lectures, a model of Dickinsonian compactness. He says more in those 52 pages than most writers say in 400.

Grant the elucidator, the enucleator, the translator, the man who ferried Heidegger to Canada, who slingshot intellectual Europe across the sea. Is that all? He certainly doesn't transfix you with strangeness the way Lispector does, so conservative in his elegant Victorian sentences. The message is a simple one: conserve

X: Obedience

the honey of the past, and chase away the hornets from the hive. He uses the New Testament and Simone Weil to chase away the amorality of Heidegger and the manic-despair of Nietzsche.

Grant doesn't change much in his thinking. What he starts with he ends with. He opens a gate. Closes a gate. Believes.

He says big things, bold things, unequivocal things: "to use the language of fate is to assert that all human beings come into a world they did not choose and live their lives within a universe they did not make" (the William Christian biography).

The biography is dedicated to Dennis Lee and Charles Taylor, a poet and a journalist. Grant dedicated *English-speaking Justice* to Lee and Alex Colville, a poet and a painter.

For me, the most exciting and evocative essay on Grant's work remains Lee's "Grant's Impasse" in *Body Music*.

The third time I met Grant—or shared space with him—was in the McMaster swimming pool. He used to go in around noon for a dip. He'd jump in the deep end and tread water—no swimming—just treading water, and he'd do that for twenty minutes or so, get out, dry himself off, and leave. I used to watch him. Ostensibly I was swimming, but really I was watching. Something about treading water has stuck in my head after twenty or so years. There's something incomplete, partial, pure in treading water. You're not going anywhere, you're not accomplishing anything, you're just doing, doing as a form of being, play as a form of spirit, purposeless doing/being. The water as sacrament, not to be conquered but to be participated in, partaken of. I admired what I took to be his abandon.

I come again to his notes after a long absence. I read them when they came out, or tried to. I couldn't crack the code. I wasn't familiar enough then with the Grantian lexicon. Who was "sw," for instance? I hadn't heard of Simone Weil then. The proper nouns he mentions in his notes are the proper nouns he surrounded his life with: Heidegger and Nietzsche, Leo Strauss and Karl Barth and Jacques Ellul too, Mozart and Weil above all. These were Grant's ancestors and contemporaries. His ancestors were his contemporaries.

He intended to write many books. The book on Nietzsche he sort of finished. He said that he read Nietzsche because his son had, so he could understand his son's enthusiasm better. He intended to write a book on Heidegger. He had a picture of Heidegger on his desk, and his biographer says when he was upset with "the old bastard" he'd put his face to the wall. He intended, above all, to write a book about Simone Weil, the saint and intellectual. Did Weil help him wed the Greeks to Christianity, Plato to Christ? Weil taught him that intellect unilluminated by love is a hollow thing. He was late in explicitly acknowledging her, though she had been there almost from the beginning. For awhile she was the unmentioned one, a bit like the Holy Spirit. You can't see her directly in most of the

X: Obedience

writing but she's there; you can feel her presence. At the end, Grant talked about her freely, in his review of her work in *The Globe and Mail*, in the conversations with CBC broadcaster David Cayley, in his final unfinished notes.

Maybe when someone is really close to you there is no need to talk about her. She's just there: like air, like light, like love.

Obedience. Can you think of anything more bizarre to write about in our time than obedience? To what or to whom would we be obedient? What or whom do we reverence enough, stand in awe of enough, to proffer obedience? What could be more anti-historical, ahistorical, than obedience?

It's what Heidegger lacked. He never met a mind larger than his own. He recognized no one to whom he would submit or surrender, no one to kneel before; he thought primarily within the cosmic sphere, not the human sphere—more about Being than beings. Grant stays within the human fold of being, with beings. He has great regard for Heidegger's meditative thought, his ability to see into an object without splitting it. Heidegger could let things be. He wanted to let Being and beings be. Maybe that's a kind of obedience—to let each being simply be. Be itself. Be what it's here for. A bird's here for flying. Let it fly. A fish is here for swimming. Let it swim. What's a person here for? For thought? for love? for their confluence?

Yes, the kind of obedience Grant talks about Heidegger didn't have, obedience within the human sphere. Obedience to a person. Heidegger would not doff his hat to his ancestors, not to Plato, not to Nietzsche, not to Christ. And yet, maybe Grant needed to rethink this. Heidegger would stand in awe of Being and reverence the power that bodies forth. The power/the ground that potentially presences. The power that gives. Man, for Heidegger, ought to be the guardian of Being, the shepherd of Being, even the voice of Being. There's a kind of obedience there, even a response to a call. Grant insists, though:

> what is the divide
>
> that n & h seem to have crossed about good?
>
> There are still goods for n
>
> & in some sense for h.
>
> but what there is not for them is obedience
>
> the question then
>
> is what is taken out of the word good
>
> when you use it without the presence of obedience
>
> & what is told us of the word good
>
> when we use it with the word obedience.

Mozart, says Grant, had obedience. "His music is obedience." He attends to the whole.

> obedience is 1st to X.
>
> & who or what is X.?

– X: Obedience –

> we are called to obedience to X.
>
> because he is obedience
>
> X is the perfection presented to us
>
> of the offering up of himself to good
>
> to good which commands obedience

You get a taste of Grant's mind here, its reach, its movement. He's a questioner, a definer. He thinks in clusters, in bunches, each thought joined to another on a common vine. What does a sisterword lose when you deprive it of its motherword? What does a sisterword gain in communion with its motherword? Obedience is related to Christ who is related to the good.

Grant's definition of religion: "what men bow down to."

And grace? "Grace simply means that the great things of our existing are given us, not made by us and finally not to be understood as arbitrary accidents." A sentence to live by and be obedient to.

Grant's most powerful insight: the given overwhelms the made. There is more given in the world than is made in the world; we ourselves are more given than made. This, the one thought he was utterly obedient to: the power and the glory of the Given. The Given which is given by grace, by God. The fitting response is gratitude, and the will to give back to others—to give oneself away. In a giving universe, give, give, give.

Give away all of who you are. Society: a reciprocity of gifts, a potluck dinner, a potlatch quilt.

Once in Zambia I refused to give a friend a pair of boots. Twenty-five years later I gave a woman a hat in an open-air market in Havana. The hat lessened the intensity of the gnawing memory of the boots; the debt had been paid. I felt free. Life had given me a second opportunity to give, to relive an experience and not to fail this time... Give because you are given to... Give because you are a gift... Give.

Thomas Merton's short meditation on the begging bowl of the Buddha:

> It represents the ultimate theological root of the belief, not just in a right to beg, but in openness to the gifts of all beings as an expression of the interdependence of all beings...when the monk begs...he is simply opening himself to this interdependence.

To be as open as a bowl, as interdependent as a dog (Artie, Grant's "dear companion for 17 years").

"The highest human life is to give oneself away," says Grant. That's what Grant wanted to be able to do—to give himself away. Weil again and further back, Paul, and further back, Christ.

Like Nietzsche and Heidegger, all his life Grant was an etymologist, tracking the origins and tracing the shifts of the word. He enucleates; he separates the wheat

– X: Obedience –

from the chaff, the seed from the tree; and replants. Tradition, Grant says in the Massey lectures, is a handing over—a surrender.

Grant's definition of thought: "steadfast attention to the whole." Did he know D.H. Lawrence's lines? "Thought is not a trick, or an exercise, or a set of dodges,/thought is a man in his wholeness wholly attending." Why didn't he read more poetry?

David Cayley, at the end of his introduction to the conversations with Grant, says, "Grant was engaged in what I think is the most important task of our time: the writing of what Ivan Illich once called 'a constitution of limits.'"

That's what Heidegger lacks—limits. Because there is no obedience, there are no limits. When you obey someone, you are limited. You are, in Paul's theological language, "a prisoner of the Lord."

"Mastery means masterlessness" says Grant in his notes on obedience. Even intellectual mastery? Especially intellectual mastery. Grant in conversation with Cayley says "the idea of limit to me is the idea of God."

Grant lived and wrote by limits. He refused publicly to say anything that might be construed as negative against Judaism for fear anti-Semites might use his words to vilify; he was reluctant to criticize the Catholic church for fear such criticism might assist the further division of Christendom. Time and again in David Cayley's *George Grant in Conversation* he says: I can't speak about that...because I'm not there yet... I'm not ready... I don't know enough...

William Christian, in *George Grant: A Biography*, quotes Grant as saying: "You'll remember that in 509b of *The Republic* Plato says that the Good is beyond being. Therefore what divides Platonists from the Aristotelians is that Aristotelians say that the fundamental question is the question of Being and the Platonists say that it is the question of Good." The Good lies behind/beyond Being. But "the language of good may have gone/so how does one perform the job" (Grant in his notes on obedience). His great fear was that the old language was too deeply buried and the new language was too far removed from flesh and blood to move towards clarity and charity, language fast being replaced by mathematics and symbolic logic as the height of human aspiration and longing.

Enter faith. Christian retells Grant's epiphany. In England. A country road. Riding his bike. A gate across the road. Gets off his bike. Opens the gate. Goes through. Shuts the gate. Believes. In a wink of an eye, "God is."

The epiphany occurs after exhausting work in air raid shelters during the blitz in London. Grant witnesses the deaths of friends, and has feelings of great helplessness. He is witness to mutilated bodies and the rending of souls. He has what his family calls "a nervous breakdown."

How often in the history of conversion is there an accompanying helplessness, weakness, breakdown? Paul is thrown to the ground by a great light.

X: Obedience

From that day in December 1941, speaking of what he learned in that experience, Grant says: "the recognition that I am not my own."

Where Being is Goodness is.

> thought is under obedience
>
> h denies this
>
> you wish to assert this
>
> thought is free to roam
>
> and say what h says
>
> when it is free from obedience
>
> the greatest writer on what technique is
>
> turns his back on obedience

Grant thought within limits, thought under obedience, thought responsive to a call. Consider his thought that

> thinking is perhaps the best good of goods—
>
> but it is not the supreme good
>
> or the total good.

What's higher? Love. Intellect, in Simone Weil's phrase, illuminated by love; intellect summoned to obedience.

Grant puts limits to his thoughts, reins them in, only too mindful of Swift—that thought can be spider-like and make webs or it can be bee-like and make honey.

The deconstructionists make webs; they are the spiders of our time. They treat life and learning as objects, that which is thrown away from us, removed, distant enough from the heart to be a game, an amusement, something to snicker at; they subvert, make ironies of everything so as to make themselves impregnable—Nietzsche's will-to-power taken to the nth degree. Let them deconstruct themselves. The human enterprise has always been about construction, about the making of honey for sweetness and light.

Grant's challenge to the poet Lee: make honey.

In the postmodern theorists, there is an absence of honey. In postmodernity, there is no honey in the hive. The world is a set of objects for scrutiny and mastery. Do not underestimate human self-loathing.

Grant persisted in his fear of a museum culture in which the traditions of the past, the bee's honey, would be webbed over by the spider's entrails. World Wide Web.

His fight at McMaster was to ensure that the Department of Religion study religion from the viewpoint of a believer, not as a museum piece.

Can I understand anyone or anything without love, without belief in their goodness? Can I know my bullheaded Golden Retriever without loving him? If I don't love him, isn't he merely number and biological process? Without love, the world is number and process. Can I love without obedience? Without giving from and emptying into obedience?

X: Obedience

> duty & delight in farrer
>
> i do not get what i thought about prayer
>
> because i always turn away from it
>
> because i know i am not willing to give myself away
>
> how much is mozartian tragedy & sadness
>
> the response of giving oneself away?
>
> but then think of the last movement of 503

Sometimes the Good in Grant can't be said or understood but it can always be heard—in music, in Mozart, "the lute of God."

Go to where the voice is. Go to the voices you need. The ones you hear faintly, in murmur, the ones that demand obedience.

> obedience is not an easy thing
>
> thought & obedience—
>
> —modern thought has darkened obedience
>
> what strauss misses are the saints
>
> yet obedience is dark...
>
> n thought that transcendence was extinguished
>
> i think that it is darkened, as a believer.
>
> But that one can think transcendence easily
>
> is just not so

Grant was concerned with the Good, and the Good "was what we were suited for." Are we suited for obedience? Or, like Prometheus and Adam, are we born to rebel? The parable of the Prodigal Son connects the two: no real obedience without rebellion first.

Grant was suited for re-firing some old words: grace, goodness, limits, obedience. Perhaps everyone is born to fumigate a few words; give a word or two personal inflection and accent.

Grant tried to put the horizon back into human dwelling on earth, the horizon taken out by Nietzsche and Heidegger. Grant the restorer, the resuscitator, the obedient one. He lived obedience to thought under the command of love, an obedience incarnated by Christ.

His mission as a thinker: to think obediently.

XI
Mercy

Poems. All his life poems. Well-made, half-made, badly made. Bits and pieces, snapshots and shards. All songs—satirical, parodic, spoofing, elegiac, lyrical, Zenny, Beat, prosaic—singed with a very human breath. Thomas Merton gathers words into poems and converts spirit into flesh.

A poet has the right to sing, even if off key, even if out of tune. And sometimes those half-sung, half-breath songs hopscotch into a more human chord than hymns to form and finesse. Sometimes the rough-hewn stones seem more stone-like than polished gems, and poems as common as daisies, as comforting as robins, seem more thirsted for than Olympian oracles.

> I think poetry must
>
> I think it must
>
> Stay open all night
>
> In beautiful cellars

He does have some good ones: "An Elegy for Ernest Hemingway," "For My Brother: Reported Missing in

Action, 1943," "Love Winter When the Plant Says Nothing," "Night-Flowering Cactus," "Song for Nobody." But it's not until his creative adaptation of Chuang Tzu that Merton finds his full-throated ease in someone else's song: *The Way of Chuang Tzu* and the way of Thomas Merton, a magnificent palimpsest, a forgetting of the self and a finding it in another.

Even so, even allowing for this happy marriage between an old sage and a new suitor, Merton's best poetry frequently slums in his prose. Hear again that unforgettable first sentence of *The Seven Storey Mountain*: "On the last day of January 1915, under the sign of the Water Bearer, in a year of a great war, and down in the shadow of some French mountains on the borders of Spain, I came into the world."

The sentence has the checked energy, the zigzag movement of a Hemingway line cast like a fly on the water, thrown out and pulled back; it quivers between the stateliness and mock-grandeur associated with a line from Swift; and it leaves the most important revelation to the end in the manner of Milton. (These three writers, by the way, Merton had just been reading or teaching at Saint Bonaventure University before taking up the pen for his first full-scale autobiography.)

In *Chuang Tzu*, the master of the marginal—of letters, journals and meditations—jigs and reels at his poetic best when not trying to be poetic. Thomas Merton and the Chinese sage put it this way: "When the archer is shooting for nothing/He has all his skill."

XI: Mercy

Dreams. Dreams of women all his life. "I dreamt I was sitting with a very young Jewish girl of fourteen or fifteen, and that she suddenly manifested a very deep and pure affection for me and embraced me so that I was moved to the depths of my soul. I learned that her name was 'Proverb,' which I thought very simple and beautiful… I spoke to her of her name, and she did not seem to be proud of it, because it seemed that the other girls mocked her for it. But I told her it was a very beautiful name…" All this Merton tells Boris Pasternak. Years later he dreams of another girl, or the same girl. "Last night I had a haunting dream of a Chinese princess which stayed with me all day. ('Proverb' again.) She comes to me in various mysterious ways in my dreams. This time she was with her 'brothers,' and I felt overwhelmingly the freshness, the youth, the wonder, the truth of her… Yet I deeply felt the sense of her understanding, knowing and loving me, in my depths…"

Sometimes Merton lived at zero, and dreamt his way out.

Memories. His American Quaker mother was strict. In his mind, aloof. And yet she recorded everything about him. Mother his first biographer; the biography called *Tom's Book*. At age two he had 16 teeth, was 34 inches tall, weighed 30 pounds, and had a vocabulary of 160 words, many of which were bird names. Mother's narcissism engendered his? The word "colour" he associated with his father, an abstract painter from New Zealand. Jenkins and Merton were Welsh names.

Mother died when he was six. She wrote him a letter to say that she was dying of cancer. She chose not to tell him in person. He felt broken and rejected. When his father formed a close friendship with another woman and spent his time painting and travelling and cavorting with her, Merton felt rejected again. He didn't see much of his younger brother.

Mothers. White mothers, black mothers. What does it mean to dream of a "black mother"? "And there she was. Her face was ugly and severe, yet a great warmth came from her to me and we embraced in love. I felt deep gratitude… Then we danced a little together, I and my black mother."

Lost and found. Merton knew about loss. He knew about orphanhood. By his late teens he had lost his mother, his father, his brother, his grandparents. He lost a woman during the war years by whom he had a child. Later he lost M, the nurse with whom he fell in love in a Louisville hospital. He lost a country (France), though not its language; he lost a career (teaching English). He found a friend—the poet Robert Lax—and kept him. Merton always kept his friends. He hung onto them by the only means he could: by letter. Letters were his cable to the world. He found a religion: Catholicism. He found a vocation: Cistercian monasticism. He found a task: to undergo changes and transformations and to write about himself in a state of change and transformation in such a way that the reader wonders if he is part of the transformation too. The

— XI: Mercy —

Merton magic is that in transforming himself he transforms you.

Jean Leclercq: "We are now discovering that there was not one Merton, but several successive or simultaneous ones."

Orphanhood. The orphan chooses an orphan form: autobiography. His life's work, one of the longest ongoing autobiographies in the century, primarily in journal form. Who is he? He's a magazine editor (*Monk's Pond*), a poet and a friend to poets, a photographer, a calligrapher, a drawer, a writer, a teacher, a sayer of prayers, a presider of the Eucharist, a wood-chopper, a bourbon-drinker, a cheese-eater, a monk, a hermit, a translator. He translates the monastery to the world and the world to the monastery; he translates silence into words and words into silence; he translates from the Latin, from the Greek, from the Persian, even from the Chinese (with the help of his friend John Wu); he translates Pessoa, Vallejo, Char, Cardenal, Cuadra—great poets of the century.

Names. Names. The Portuguese poet Pessoa had four. Kierkegaard had seven or eight. Swift had dozens. Masks. Disguises. Extensions. Multiple identities. Merton had scores of pseudonyms he used in corresponding with his friends, from Wang and Homer to Joey the Chocolate King and Frisco Jack.

His name in Chinese means "Silent Lamp." In Persian he's "simurgh," "the King of the soaring birds." In the *I Ching* he's the wanderer, fire over mountain.

His day. He reveals his daily life as a hermit to a Sufi scholar, Abdul Aziz, in a letter dated January 2, 1966 (available in *The Hidden Ground of Love*, letters selected and edited by William H. Shannon). Merton informs Aziz that he goes to bed at 7:30 at night and gets up about 2:30 in the morning. Upon rising he says part of the canonical Office consisting of psalms and lessons. He meditates for an hour and a quarter. He does some Bible reading. He makes tea or coffee and sometimes has a fruit or honey breakfast. With breakfast he begins reading and studying until sunrise. At sunrise he says another Office of psalms. He then begins manual work consisting of sweeping, cleaning and cutting wood. If he has time, he writes a few letters. He then goes to the monastery to say Mass. After Mass he has a cooked meal in the monastery. Returning to the hermitage, which is about half a mile's walk from the monastery, he reads, says another Office, and meditates for about an hour. He then writes for a couple of hours. By now it's late afternoon. He says another Office of psalms and prepares himself a light supper, usually soup and a sandwich with a cup of tea. Dishes are kept to a minimum. After supper he meditates for another hour and then goes to bed.

One of his prose-poem tracts he entitles "Day of A Stranger." A stranger unto himself.

– XI: Mercy –

His day: controlled and wild, regimented and free, ritualistic, ceremonial. Of chant and silence, of cheese and fire, of prayer and wakefulness made. Awake in the night, defying the dark. The seasons passing rhythmically from one to another, beyond the Order's hand.

For all his rambunctiousness and his changeability, he remained disciplined and obedient to his calling.

His journey, exterior. "From Prades to Bermuda to St. Antonin to Oakham to London to Cambridge to Rome to New York to Columbia to Corpus Christi to St. Bonaventure to the Cistercian Abbey of the poor men who labor in Gethsemani." The sands of geography shift, so he can learn to know "[The] mercy which has created [him]..." and "the Christ of the burnt men." His journey, interior. "It's a matter of growth, of deepening, and an ever growing surrender to the creative action of love and grace in our hearts." A surrender to mercy.

Key words. Words you open by; words you're opened by. Merton's key words:

fire (he dies "a General Electric death," fire imagery abounds in the poetry, one of his loveliest prose tracts "Fire Watch");

mountains (he's born under the shadow of a mountain, Kanchenjunga his last great mountain seen);

desert (where the silence and solitude come from);

seeds (of contemplation and speculation); and

mercy (the open-heart, the hidden pulse of the universe giving and receiving, creating and destroying).

These are his master metaphors, his lifewords, hovering over him like night stars. And the one guiding North Star: mercy. "The plants hold themselves up on stems which have a single consistency, that of mercy, or rather great mercy... In the formlessness of night and silence a word then pronounces itself: Mercy."

The poem to Kerouac, Alice Notley's "Jack Would Speak through the Imperfect Medium of Alice," fits Merton too.

> Every me I was & wrote
>
> were only & all (gently)
>
> That one perfect word

The one perfect word—mercy. In *Fire Watch*, July 4, 1952, he repeats the word three times: "Mercy within mercy within mercy."

Mercy for his guilt, for his feeling lucky, for living when others died. Mercy for things done and undone, things said and unsaid. Mercy for being difficult and being troubled, mercy for a good life.

Merton the word man: words from newspapers, from ads, from scholarly journals, from esoteric Bud-

XI: Mercy

dhist texts. The man made of words. Merton the bookman. He hauls bags of books with him to Asia, and pays overweight charges for the privilege of excess. A reader of books, a writer of books. His vow of conversation is a sacred vow in his silent order. Merton the noisiest, most raucous Trappist in the history of Christendom. Over 60 books, journals still pouring out. Over 4,000 letters. Over 250 essays. Hundreds of poems, numbering over 1,000 pages. His literary output is as vast as Raymond Carver's and Kristjana Gunnars' is small.

How to become a Catholic? Read Blake, Joyce, Traherne, Hopkins. Merton did. Have a literary conversion. Simone Weil did. She was converted by George Herbert. How to become a Zen Buddhist? Meditate. Laugh a lot. Merton as Zen Beat poet, creator of anti-worlds: anti-poems, anti-letters, anti-novels.

Shrunk by a shrink. Dr. Zilboorg diagnoses him "verbological." An incessant babbler. He wants to take him off words the way a detox counsellor wants to take a man off booze. Says he could only be alone in New York City, only quiet in Grand Central Station with a sign above his begging bowl and blanket, "Hermit lives here."

Once Joan Baez dropped in, and he danced a little jig for her. Drank a little bourbon. He hooted and spun like a Dervish at the thought she might take him to see his student-nurse M.

Every life a quarry from which you only extract a few stones. A life is what you live and fail to live, what you dream about, what surrounds you. Tone a matter of geography as much as psychology. A physical positioning side-wagoned to a mental attitude. Where are you when you're speaking? Are you above me, below me, beside me? Merton walks alongside you, talking as he walks.

Everybody's a character from Shakespeare. Merton's Hamlet. Self-confessions, self-chidings, self-pep talks, self-flagellations, self-inspirations. Soliloquies to himself, asides to others. Sometimes Merton is Hamlet crossed with Holden Caulfield. He can see through phoniness.

A frugal death: 1 Timex watch, in the estimation of the Bangkok police worth ten dollars. The other items—1 pair dark glasses in tortoise frames, 2 pairs bifocal eyeglasses in plastic frames, 2 Cistercian leather-bound breviaries, 1 rosary (broken), 1 small icon on wood of Virgin and Child—all judged to be nil in material value.

Form. He wrestles with form all his life. By 1968, the year of his death, he'd found it. "Forget form, and it suddenly appears, ringed and reverberating with its own light… Well, then: stop seeking. Let it all happen. Let it come and go. What? Everything: ie., nothing." Clarice Lispector would understand these lines.

His long book-length poems at the end of his life—*Cables to the Ace* and *The Geography of Lograire*—find their form; it just takes awhile to enter into their spirit, and see the macro-order over the mini-chaos of individual lines and stanzas. These are poems you wait for, a poetics you wade into slowly.

The last poems. For these, "this wide-angle mosaic of poems and dreams," the less understanding the better. He's working on what I like to call a Book of Strange. These last books of poetry are strange, strange in content, strange in tone. Clarice Lispector might have written them if she had been a poet.

> Come go green slow dark maps green late home
>
> Should long beach death night ever come
>
> And welcome to dark father-mother land
>
> Simple white wall house square rock hill
>
> Green there low water hill rock square
>
> White home in dark bituminous con-
>
> Crete ways to plain of fates ways
>
> Fathers hill and green maps memory plain
>
> In holy green Wales there is never staying

Who's speaking? A Dickinsonian question. Why is he speaking this way? A joining mind, Merton's, a mind jumping and connecting, a "mind leaping like dolphins," a mind that can solder rain and a rhinoceros.

These last poems are odd cables. Strange geographies, histories, biographies, autobiographies, anthropologies, poetries, mythologies, Ghost Dances and Cargo Cults served up in a Joycean mishmash, with diamonds in the slag.

> Slowly slowly
>
> Comes Christ through the garden
>
> Speaking to the sacred trees
>
> Their branches bear his light
>
> Without harm

Merton had begun to remake himself again in these final cables. He's singing a new song. And for a new song he needs a new self. He succeeds in making himself new again, fresh again, strange to himself again.

> But birds fly uncorrected across burnt lands
>
> The surest home is pointless:
>
> We learn by the cables of orioles.

His thoughts are driven into form, trailored to a beat, scattered and regathered, careening off again into new orbits, bouncy and sad, a laugh and a tear clip-clopping through it all.

By *The Asian Journal*, no privileging, all human. Merton in that last spontaneous scribble has found his form, everything coming at you at once with the same weight and dignity, prose on the run, poetry on the spot. He's working in the quick. The journal consists of poems and photographs, lists and impressions, commentaries and predictions; he weaves loose on the loom.

– XI: Mercy –

The ambivalence of writing. He tries to give up writing when he first enters the monastery. He bunkers down, narrows himself, tries to disappear. He soon tires of that. Then he broadens and reaches out and embraces everything. "Some conclusions: Literature, contemplative solitude, Latin America, Asia, Zen, Islam etc., all these things come together in my life. It would be madness for me to attempt to create a monastic life for myself by excluding all these."

Photographs. Not an inconsiderable photographer himself. See "Cloister Niche"—with its apparition like a third person—"White Chair," "Stone Wall," "Cleft Rock," "Birds," "Mt. Kanchenjunga," "Tibetan Child," all Shaker-simple, all in *The Geography of Holiness*.

John Howard Griffin, the author of *Black Like Me*, took some good photographs of him, so did Jim Forrest the peace activist, and so did the photographer Ralph Eugene Meatyard. Meatyard's photographs are deliberately blurred, out of focus, catching the movement in the stillness. Merton surrounded by books. Merton reading and writing. Merton with bongo drums. Merton hamming it up outside a barn. Merton surrounded by poet-friends. Merton taking photographs of the photographer. Merton sitting: alone, quiet, still, in the dark. And beneath one photograph, Meatyard's simple description: "Early winter 1967, meal—cheese, bread, wine, talk 3 hours." Mercifully simple. Simple mercy.

XII
Whither the Word?

There are things I haven't told you. In any story, isn't there always more untold than told? For example: Clarice Lispector quotes Thomas Merton in her journalism. Dennis Lee quotes him in the Nightwatch sequence of his selected poems. Merton identified Dickinson as his "own flesh and blood," a "quiet rebel," who had no truck in "catchwords and formalities." He regarded Flannery O'Connor as a modern Sophocles. He never stopped reading D.H. Lawrence. My writers have secret intercourse with each other; their signature words migrate freely.

Have I told you that my ambition is to write something like Merton's *Asian Journal,* something as wild and mixed and chaotic? Or that my mind balked once after too much Heidegger and again after too much Lispector and Dickinson? Like a horse that had run too far for its strength, my mind said, "This far. No farther." With Merton I just feel so very comfortable. I breathe easy with him.

I've been thinking about Merton, and writing on his work, for something like sixteen years. I've written about him in *The Merton Annual, The Merton Seasonal,*

Kentucky Poetry Review, Brick, The Antigonish Review, The Globe and Mail, Kairos, Grail... I own a small library of books by and about him. He won't go away. He looks down impishly upon me in my study, denim jacket over cassock, his hand underlining a script. I write under his smiling face and humble prayers. A favourite begins: "My Lord God, I have no idea where I am going..." You've got to like a guy who daily faces his measure of confusion head-on.

I keep trying to say goodbye to him. It's time to move on. You can't spend your life with a single poet-monk, can you? No sooner do I throw him out than he boomerangs back. Mostly it's his voice that seduces me. The voice of intimacy. The voice of pain. The voice of honesty.

Middle to late Merton speaks to you as if he were you or you were he or you and he were one. He speaks brother to brother, brother to sister. He cracks open Ursula Le Guin's bipolarity of the father tone and the mother tone with a third option: the brother-sister tone. He doesn't lecture from the pulpit (dad) or banter from the kitchen (mom); he talks freely at the table where siblings are seated.

He shows you his wounds in words as simple as bread, as full-bodied as wine. When he finishes talking, you ask yourself: is he talking about himself or about me?

I need his voice. I need his word too. Mercy. Mercy for being so damn lucky when others whom I love have been burdened by heavy sacks of sorrow.

– XII: Whither the Word? –

There are other things I haven't told you. I haven't told you that Cheryl and I like to watch Italian and Chinese movies, movies in just about any language except English. We like not to understand fully, not to know. We like the strangeness of being overwhelmed and swept away. Gong Li is the most beautiful actress in the world. Have I told you that?

I wonder if you can feel my presence at all. I feel small, like a Kristjana Gunnars' book. Hardly here at all. I'm made of words, made from the Other, made from the words of the Other. I think she is too, and that's why I emotionally connect with her work. My house is built neither on rock nor sand but on voice. What's here is my voice—my breath, my breathing, my words. Wordwinds.

Words move with the quick or not at all. Their movement depends on how much body-breath you can get in. Words are alive or dead. I want Lawrentian life pulsing through every syllable I utter. Sometimes that happens, and sometimes it doesn't. This I know: there's no way of manipulating the quick. It's not to be bargained for or negotiated with. It's there or not there; it comes and goes.

I haven't fallen to zero yet. Not once have I truly lived in the basement where Dickinson spent most of her mental life. I have friends who have lived at zero and who have found the strength to crawl out. Me, I've lived in the attic, with the wind blowing in my hair. Blessings have followed me like the moon at night. More to feel guilty about.

Have I given you enough? O'Connor gives you everything she has, everything she is: all her crusty uncompromising clarity, all her shattering insight into human pretension and deception. At one point she must have been struck by lightning—just as Dickinson and Lispector were and Carver was in "Cathedral"—to have seen so much. Such Damascus Road revelation hasn't come my way yet, at least not as dramatically as it came to Merton in an old church in Havana, on Fourth and Walnut in Louisville, and in Polinnaruwa. Nor has it come as absolutely as it came to Flannery O'Connor, that fierce Catholic writer of Irish descent. I wait.

Being, even after Heidegger's unparalleled elucidation, still stumps me. It's still a mystery. It's still, in the word I associate with Clarice Lispector, strange. What is it that wants to come forth, to be present, to make its presence known and why? I do feel myself, like Raymond Carver in his last years, to be surrounded and blessed by love. I remember Tess Gallagher's words about him in a poem—"Did he mean never to be thought of apart/from love?"—and hope that Cheryl will never think of me apart from love.

I still chafe at obedience. I tend to like the first seven letters of the word protestant. Protest: protest authority, laws, rules, habits, expectations, givens. My paternal grandfather was an Orangeman. He wore the sash his father wore. But my father didn't. He refused to join the Order. He protested. If I'm loyal, if I'm obedient, I'm inclined to be obedient first to my father's rebellion.

– XII: Whither the Word? –

There's a secret I want to share. While I've been writing, I've been listening to Bob Dylan. "Gotta serve somebody." I've just come back from the city of my birth where I had the privilege of seeing Dylan live with Van Morrison at the Botanic Gardens. Part of a European tour. That's what Dylan opened with: "Y' gonna hafta serve somebody."

Grant would have agreed. Merton too. He used to play Dylan, loudly, in the hermitage. One of his last unfinished projects was to write an article on Dylan's songs. Lee, a man of night songs and simple songs, would agree too, though he might be uncomfortable with the "somebody."

Many serve the god of change on this planet. I'm not sure what god I serve. Maybe the god of no-name. The word I've been using throughout for the holy is Spirit. It names without naming. Breath. Wind. Voice. These are some of its attributes. Change too, I guess, but change in the soul, not just in the skin.

Yes, there are things I haven't told you. I first met Dennis Lee years ago in a Korean Zen Temple in north Toronto. He had come, as I and hundreds of others had, to hear a Vietnamese Buddhist monk, the one whom Merton called brother. The talk went on for three and a half hours. The monk talked. Rang a bell. Fell into silence. Then he asked people to breathe in the good and breathe out the bad. He was teaching us how to breathe. Then he resumed his talk, and repeated the pattern. A talk with bells. Speech and silence struck in a single, snake-entwined note.

Of all the words I've quarried, the one spiritbookword I feel closest to is Lee's word tremendum: its odd sound, its foreign look. I need something to close my eyes to. Something to bow down to. Something that makes me shiver. The feeling of tremendum I get mostly from reading books. But I get it too from witnessing small acts of kindness. My son once admired my father's leather coat. My father took it off immediately and gave it to him. Each smiled affectionately at the other. I was in tremendum over an old man's generosity and a young man's gratitude.

I talk to myself, and argue. I'm still wrestling with my three-in-one: Spirit. Book. Word. Can you have one without the others as sidekicks? What's a book? Keeper of the word. And a word? Preserver of spirit. And spirit? Breath. Yes, maybe they're a family. When Gunnars quotes Heidegger in *The Rose Garden*—"The word alone gives being to the thing"—I think she intends the spiritbookword, the word birthed in the book, the word that blows life into things. Do you still have the word if you take away its protective cover?

Will I still hear the Spirit if I don't have bookwords in which to listen for the rustle? Can the wired word strike the tuning fork of the self? Can the webbed book radiate light? Can anything other than a book make me so forgetful of time? I remember Raymond Carver's simple, honouring words in his poem "Reading:"

XII: Whither the Word?

> ...There in the window
>
> on warm and sunny days is a man
>
> so engrossed in reading he doesn't look
>
> up...

And again in "After Reading Two Towns in Provence" where he addresses the author:

> I spent the entire morning
>
> in your company in Aix,
>
> in the South of France.
>
> When I looked up,
>
> it was twelve o'clock.

One of the reasons I so much enjoy Gunnars' *Rose Garden* is how she stitches in her love of reading and her reverence for books.

> She reads not because she wishes to, but because she has to. It is necessary. She either reads or dies.

Is Gunnars speaking personally here?

> I remember the stack of books and how I dipped into them like a pool in the afternoon shade.

She quotes Proust:

> Always I was incapable of seeing anything for which a desire had not already been roused in me by something I had read.

Spirit Book Word

These words would be true for Carver and Merton, I suspect, as they seem to be true for Gunnars. They're true for me.

And so are her words:

The book that holds the world together. People will give a book to a child or a friend. It is more than a gift: it is an inspiration... The gift of soul, something that grows with time and does not get used up.

What a beautiful definition of a book! A gift of soul. Something that grows and doesn't get used up.

Maybe I'm a Jurassic who feels uncomfortable if I can't hold in my hands what I love. Maybe that's it: the tactility of the book makes it precious to me. What I can't hold and carry feels foreign to me, as if it doesn't belong to me. Cheryl reminds me of how I liked to carry the children everywhere, and the dog too, way past the time to let them walk by themselves.

I don't know why the book and I bonded. It was an object I could hold and carry, keep and go back to, unlike friends, who, in my early years, tended to disappear. Reading for me is looking for friends and spending time with them. And what I love I want to pass on. I find myself repeating lines my daughter wrote when she was ten: "I hope everybody in this world today/ Will at least read a book some day." Yet I also believe Marshall McLuhan's truism to be accurate: what we make, remakes us.

XII: Whither the Word?

The computer remakes us by remaking what we're made of: words. It remakes our insides; it's a mindbox which not only contains our mind but what we have to transcend our mind—language. It's a wordbox. As Heidegger put it, "...the language machine [the computer] takes language into its management and thus masters the essence of the human being."

The old technology of the book issues forth from the mother of quietness and the father of stillness, but things are noisy and fast now. We're all a little wired: too much sugar in our diets, too many thoughts in our heads. It's physically difficult for kids to sit still, to be quiet, when their bodies are programmed for movement. It's psychically difficult for me to be still when my monkey mind swings from thought to thought.

Maybe I've read too much George Grant. I find myself asking: what is lost in the new superseding the old? What intimations of deprival do I hear? Technology and reverence seem to clash. Can you have a technology of reverence? Yes, the book. The book encourages reverence.

If vast vocabularies of reverence fall into disuse or are merely data amongst data or are so phantom-like as to lack logic and practical sense and are therefore unprogrammable, where do the higher spiritual aspirations of the human tribe go? What happens to the nature diction of the storyteller and poet from Nazareth? If the young don't read, or they read only facts and fantasies on a computer screen, where does the new generation of solitary outlaws come from? Whither the word without the book?

Before his death, Anthony Burgess described our "newspeak" as technological cant mixed with infantilism, the sort of talk you hear from astronauts' lips: techno-gaga. Language itself, as Heidegger predicted, may become merely an information system as opposed to fulfilling its historic role as the generator of human dreams.

What I fear losing in such an eventuality is a voice in the writing that speaks to me personally through its rhythms and cadences, its images and metaphors, its pitch and inflection. The voice of Lispector and Merton, the voice of Dennis Lee's personas, and the voice in Kristjana Gunnars' rose garden. Outside the range of spontaneous speech, there may be sounds you can reach only through the practised and rehearsed word, the bookword.

Are there places images cannot go and states of being they cannot realize?

In the scheme of things, the possible eclipse of the book and even the word's absorption into the computer-sponge may be a minor loss compared to the loss of plants and animals. Still, it matters to me that I may not be able to hear certain sounds, swish and melodic, like rare notes on a harpsichord seldom sounded. It matters that certain words may fall off the language-band, that we may be entering a new Orwellian newspeak in which the only real words are the ones that don't look out of place on a computer screen.

– XII: Whither The Word? –

Sometimes, in such moods, I feel in the pit of my stomach the onrush of monoculture, monoword and monobeing. I hear Dylan's piercing lines: "Don't even hear the murmur of a prayer./It's not dark yet./But it's gettin' there."

You and I may fast be entering Picasso's *Guernica*, in which our spirit-selves are severed from our animal-selves—blood aflow, limbs akimbo, mouths agape, carnage all around, millennial cables connecting us to nature and to ourselves irretrievably cut. We have certainly entered Book Three of *Gulliver's Travels* where human gadgetry now overwhelms human animality. The toys seem more interesting than the toy-makers.

We are perhaps becoming some hybrid Greek creature long ago dreamt of—a sphinx, with an electronic head and an animal body. We may even be approaching the Body Electric that B.W. Powe in *Outage* brings to life: a globally pulsing-flashing-beeping-humming spider trapped in the webwork of its own making, screaming for release.

Perhaps I overdramatize.

To be fair, there are moments of splendour in the new media when old words take on fresh currency. I remember, for example, watching Krzystof Kieslowski's *Blue* and feeling—chorally, orchestrally, by Polish and by English—the full weight of Paul's sublime love letter to the Corinthians, a passage I have read dozens of times without similar emotion. I wept at the voices of the choir, at the cresting waves of music from the orchestra, at the strangeness of the Polish words and even at the familiar yellow English subtitles marching across the screen. The experience of multimedia rejuvenated musty words for me. I was in tremendum.

Sometimes films do wonders for words. I think of Greenaway's *Pillow Book*. I remember how Cavafy's "Ithaca" soared in popularity after being read on television at Jackie Kennedy's funeral, and the sales of W.H. Auden's love poetry sped up tenfold after its small exposure in the English film *Four Weddings and a Funeral*. The Italian film *Il Postino* has likewise extended the reach of Neruda's poetry.

Sometimes films do good things for the book. I think of Greenaway's salute in *Prospero's Books*. I remember film-stories like *Monsignor Quixote* and *Babette's Feast*, which seem as fine to me as the original book-stories on which they're based. Nevertheless, such moments of cinematic bliss where the word and the book have a fair hearing and aren't blindsided by the Big Screen or drowned by the Big Sound are comparatively rare.

Strangely, though, in some respects the word is not so much passing as it is morphing. With computer technologies, what Derrick de Kerckhove calls psycho-technologies, the word and the image blend into a new form: the image-word, the word as an image. It's not altogether a case of the rise of the image and the fall of the word; it's a case of spirit-level metamorphosing.

Are these not the central words of our techno-time: makeover and morph?

XII: Whither The Word?

Strangely, too, the word in some ways is moving closer to the body: just as transient, as vulnerable, as forever teetering on the edge. The word poofs out at the press of a button, as a life poofs out at the cessation of breath. Computers call up the dead—we all become a word when we die—and sometimes make them more living. They close gaps, fill emptiness, resurrect. Is the computer a resurrection machine? Maybe I do over-emphasize. The genie lives within a bodega of bottles.

The billboard word. The tongue word. The cinematic word. The televisual word. The computer word. The bookword. All are very real. All are useful forms of hosting or projecting the word. Yet for me the bookword holds a special status, different from the ink-words on the bodies of Greenaway characters that can be showered off and different from the screen-words on computers that can be touched off.

Only the book remains still and quiet. Only the book recognizes that what is contained is more important than the container. Only the book seems to know that some things cannot be contained at all. John 21:25 says, "And there are also many other things which Jesus did...even the world itself could not contain the books that should be written." John's Gospel recognizes that there is more in Christ, more love and Being and strangeness than can be put into a book.

The book lets the word speak. Without glitter or fanfare. It lets the word be. Without trumpet and tinsel.

I go on then with the faith that the Spirit moves mysteriously; it can straddle a computer chip as it can ride a robin. I go on with the Heideggerian conviction that Being is larger than what any one form of being can do to it. I go on with words in my mouth and with books in my hands, like a perplexed figure from an Edward Hopper painting.

For the moment, I honour the spirit-words writers have made flesh in their books, whether Dennis Lee's tremendum or Thomas Merton's mercy. I look for something to be obedient to, something to serve, even if it's just a word from the Word—wind from a larger Wind. I honour the word I may have stumbled on in a Toronto bookstore, the word I think I may be here to detect in others and enflesh on my own. Spiritbookword in Germanic compound. Or, Spirit Book Word, with the wind blowing.

I don't fully understand my word. I'm not sure where it leads, but I think my duty is to follow it, obey it, and be attentive to the wedding of the human spirit and the bookword at which, sometimes, the great Spirit— the Breath of our breaths—attends unexpectedly. My task for now is to praise this awkward word.

Praise. That's what every devout reader learns in humble communion with the book and the word. We readers are here to praise traces of the human spirit and track the movement of the Spirit in the bookword. And even though the book may be here only once, was it not through the book that we learned to praise full-throatedly?

– XII: Whither The Word? –

I must be careful to avoid idolatry. The word was here before the book, and will be here after it. Spirit needs neither book nor word to make Itself manifest or illuminate presence. Books may be balls of light. Sometimes. Words may be luminous letters. Sometimes. This I know: the Spirit moves through all, like a wind in an orchard. Always.

Ten Good Reads

Raymond Carver. *Where I'm Calling From: New and Selected Stories.* New York: Vintage Books, 1989.

Emily Dickinson. *The Complete Poems of Emily Dickinson.* Edited by Thomas H. Johnson. Boston: Little, Brown and Company, 1960.

George Grant. *Time As History.* Toronto: Canadian Broadcasting Corporation, 1969.

Kristjana Gunnars. *The Rose Garden: Reading Marcel Proust.* Red Deer: Red Deer College Press, 1996.

Martin Heidegger. *Poetry, Language ,Thought.* Translation and Introduction by Albert Hofstadter. New York: Harper & Row, 1971.

D.H. Lawrence. *The Complete Poems of D.H. Lawrence*. New York: The Viking Press, 1971.

Dennis Lee. *Nightwatch: New and Selected Poems*. Toronto: McClelland & Stewart, 1999.

Clarice Lispector. *The Passion According to G.H.* Translated by Ronald W. Sousa. Minneapolis: University of Minnesota Press, 1988.

Thomas Merton. *The Asian Journal of Thomas Merton*. New York: A New Directions Book, 1975.

Flannery O'Connor. *Flannery O'Connor, The Collected Works*. New York: The Library of America, 1988.

Acknowledgements

Thanks to my newspaper editors who have encouraged me to write: Jenny Jackson of *The Ottawa Citizen*, Martin Levin of *The Globe and Mail*, Andy Lamey of *The National Post* and Rob Howard of *The Hamilton Spectator*.

Thanks to my journal editors: Michael Higgins of *Grail*, where my notes on Dennis Lee's hunger and George Grant's obedience were published; George Sanderson of *The Antigonish Review*, where my work on Emily Dickinson and Kristjana Gunnars first appeared; Mary Cameron of *Quarry*, where my first writing on Dennis Lee appeared; Linda Spalding of *Brick*, for publishing earlier versions of my work on Thomas Merton and Martin Heidegger; Moya Cannon, for republishing my Heidegger in *Poetry Ireland Review* and arranging for publication of my Raymond Carver in Ireland's literary journal *Asylum*; and Bob Megans of *Kairos*, who first published my notes on D.H. Lawrence and the Quick.

Blessings on my friends: Marilyn Gear Pilling, who treated the manuscript as if it were her own, Dennis Lee, who made many valuable suggestions, Michael Higgins, B.W. Powe, Wayne Allan, Dan Pilling, Dale Behnke, Richard Giles, David Wagg, Bob Rego, Ted

Rettig, and Anne McPherson, my companion-on-the-road; on my family—Cheryl, Daniel and Rachel—who allow me dreamtime; Anne Louise Mahoney, Managing Editor at Novalis, who deftly shepherded the book through the publishing process; and Kevin Burns, Commissioning Editor at Novalis, whose love of spirit, book and word continues to inspire me.